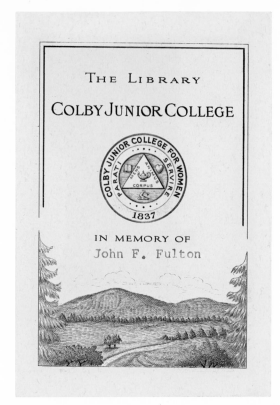

Inge Morath   From Persia to Iran

From Persia to Iran

An Historical Journey

PHOTOGRAPHS BY INGE MORATH

TEXT BY EDOUARD SABLIER

A STUDIO BOOK   THE VIKING PRESS   NEW YORK

42104

The traveler leaves for Persia, only to reach Iran. He looks forward to nightingales and roses, to a glimpse of dark eyes beneath a deftly fastened veil, and finds for the most part very ordinary people, rather glum and shabbily dressed, in very ordinary streets.

A century ago it took five months for a European to reach the capital. The French writer and diplomat Count Gobineau has left us a day-by-day account of the journey as he made it. He crossed the Mediterranean and landed in Egypt, skirted the Isthmus of Suez, and boarded a coastal steamer of the East India Company for the long, leisurely cruise down the Red Sea, across the Gulf of Aden, and up the Persian Gulf. Then began the caravan trek across the desert. Moving by easy stages past the vestiges of fifty centuries, the unhurried traveler came at last to the gardens of Shiraz and the fragrant splendors of Isfahan.

> *Wake! For the Sun who scattered into flight*
> *The Stars before him from the Field of Night,*
>   *Drives Night along with them from Heav'n, and strikes*
> *The Sultán's Turret with a Shaft of Light.*

With the opening lines of Omar Khayyám running through his mind, the traveler came, discovered, compared. By the time he had reached his journey's end, he was ready to appreciate what he found.

Today the newcomer to Iran—diplomat, businessman, or journalist—belongs as a rule to that cohort of people in a hurry who cannot or will not see for themselves. Catapulted in a single night to Tehran, he hardly moves once he gets there. His movements are limited by the political situation, by bad roads, by the lack of accommodations, or his own lack of interest; his money is running out, and so is his time.

Instead of exploring the immense country around him, he gets a glimpse of one or two cities. He has a couple of weeks in which to understand five thousand years of history.

From a brief excursion to the bazaar, where American-made products are steadily ousting those of the native craftsman, he brings back perhaps a lovely Sadjadi miniature, but more often a mere copy in cheap plastic, or mass-produced articles for sale today in every country on the globe.

Between two appointments he can't help noticing the squalor of the streets, and how few modern conveniences there are; he is struck by the absence of running water, sickened by the open "djoubs" which supply the neighboring houses with water, after being polluted by washerwomen, beggars, and dogs.

He soon finds that he can set no store by statistics. Persia is, par excellence, the land of the spoken word. Figures are unknown. The extent of the country is easy enough to compute: 628,000 square miles, the area of France, Great Britain, Spain, Italy, and Switzerland combined. But how many Persians are there? Eighteen million? Twenty-three million? No one can tell. And what about their standard of living? Where is the truth of the matter, in the complacent estimates of the Persian authorities or in the pessimistic accounts of foreigners?

How can the country be blamed for failing to provide the comforts expected by tourists? For centuries its only tourist was the invader, sweeping down from the steppes of Central Asia or the sands of Arabia, raiding, killing, pillaging, before melting away as mysteriously as he had come.

Between the happy valleys of the Indus and Mesopotamia, Iran has always been, as René Grousset aptly phrased it, "a middle empire." Its prairies and wastelands have resounded to the hoofbeats of Turanians, Macedonians, Arabs, Mongols, Turks, and Afghans. More recently still, it lay at the mercy of two gigantic empires, Russia and Great Britain, who struggled for supremacy in Iran. The contest of the Bear and the Whale, as it was called at the time, resulted periodically in a division of the spoils, the country being split into zones of influence.

In twenty-five centuries Persia has been governed by twenty-six dynasties. Only five of them were Persian. In the twelve hundred years since the advent of Mohammedanism, the country has been able to guide its own destinies for only a bare four hundred years.

"I am Darius the Great King, King of Kings, King of the lands of many races, King of this earth stretching into the distance, son of Hystaspes, of the royal family of the Achaemenidae, Persian, son of Persians, Aryan, of Aryan descent." This proud inscription is still visible at Naksh-i-Rustam. The high plateaux of Iran were settled in remote antiquity by this Aryan race which was destined to build the whole fabric of our civilization. They made their country a flourishing center of culture, art, and thought. Three thousand years before Christ the civilization of Susa extended from the Persian Gulf to the Caspian Sea. Again and again the country itself came under foreign domination, but its civilization never ceased to develop.

Iran has assimilated all its invaders. Like the white poplar of Tabriz, it has often bent in the wind, and bent low, without ever breaking. The conquerors, subdued in turn, adopted the customs of the conquered, themselves encouraging the country's rebirth. Alexander the Great died absolute master of the empire, after becoming a self-styled Iranian by proclaiming himself the successor of Darius and Xerxes. A century later the Arsacids, the Persians of the north, restored Persian unity. Shortly afterward the Sassanians, the Persians of the south, arose in turn and founded a great national empire.

Islam failed to break this continuity. About the seventh century, rotten at the core, the Sassanian empire was overrun by Arab horsemen. Iran became a province of the Caliphate, and the conqueror's religion was imposed on the length and breadth of the country.

It must have looked as if the native genius were about to be overwhelmed. But nothing of the sort happened. On the contrary, the Moslem conquest gave it a new lease of life. Iranian culture now penetrated throughout the Islamic world; in fact it became synonymous with Islam. At Bukhara, Samarkand, and Baghdad, in the Caucasus, in Egypt, in the Maghrib, even in Spain, wherever a Moslem horseman planted his standard, he was followed by Persian artists, scholars, administrators, who left the indelible mark of their civilization. A thousand years before Pasteur and Freud, Avicenna discovered microbes and psychoanalysis. Nawawi supplied the people of the steppes with a cultural tradition. Persia gave Islam its *Thousand and One Nights,* covered the Moslem lands with observatories, "medressehs," domes, and "iwans." Unlike the other Moslemized peoples, the Persians were not the poor relations of the Arab princes of the Mohammedan religion.

Assimilated though they were to Islam, the Persians retained their own personality. Faced with the Sunnite orthodoxy, they invented Shiism. While the whole Mohammedan world accepted the authority of a Caliph elected as the successor of the Prophet, the Shiites held aloof and recognized as Imam (the spiritual and temporal head of Islam) none but the direct successors of the third Caliph, Ali. By adopting Shiism, the Persians reaped many advantages. Though Moslems, they stood apart from the rest of Islam and thereby kept themselves intact instead of being engulfed. By declaring that the last Imam, the Mahdi, will remain hidden till the end of time, they reserve the right to interpret the letter and spirit of the dogma in his name, instead of submitting like other Moslems to the absolutism of tradition. Regarding all authority as illegitimate, the Persians sturdily asserted their individuality, and their individualism; and they were thus enabled, without detriment to their faith, to resist the inroads of any Moslem but non-Iranian power.

Iran has often adopted foreign ways and foreign ideas, but never without modifying them and adjusting them to its own taste and tradition. Conquests and domination have left their mark on the land but not on the individual. What was it Gobineau said of granite? "For one force that might chip it in a hundred years, a thousand would spend themselves in vain."

The cumulative effect of this unbroken tradition of getting the best of the outsider amounts to this: the average Persian today is an arch skeptic. To foreign eyes he may look like a practicing, mosque-going Moslem. Whether he is really a believer is another question. Like all the countries of Asia, Iran has always made a point of keeping its religion hidden from prying eyes. From the Mithraic mysteries and the centuries of persecution the people have learned not to make a show of their religious beliefs in public. As Gobineau put it, "What's the good of exposing your faith to the insults of unbelievers; your person, your belongings, the consideration you enjoy, to the blindness, folly, and perversity of your adversaries?"

So it is that the Persian, from time immemorial, has shrouded the metaphysics of his inner life in silence. But when silence has failed to afford protection, he has never hesitated to set his true opinions aside and heap ruse on ruse in order to outwit his opponent. Still to be found today in many an officially Moslem home are families who practice rites handed down by the Zoroastrian tradition, and Jews converted to Islam who scrupulously avoid handling fire on Saturdays. To this day in Iranian Kurdistan there are Christians who go through the ritual of prayer prescribed by the Koran.

What in the West would pass for deceit and cowardice has been regarded for centuries in Persia as a legitimate means of defense, as behavior which, by ensuring survival in this life, will entitle one to enjoy the next life promised by the Prophet. But the upshot of this system of calculated deceit is that the Persian people no longer believe and cannot be induced to believe in anything. At the end of the last war, supported by the Russian Army, the revolutionaries of Persian Azerbaijan announced the advent of a glorious new era, which they began by giving the land outright to those who tilled it and releasing the peasants from debts contracted toward their landlords. The peasants nevertheless continued regularly to set aside from their meager income the sum normally paid as rent, and no one was surprised or unprepared, after the collapse of the democratic Commune, when, as if nothing had changed, they were summoned to pay up the rent money due to the landlords.

> But helpless Pieces of the Game He plays
> Upon this Chequer-board of Nights and Days;
>   Hither and thither moves, and checks, and slays,
> And one by one back in the Closet lays.

The game of chess was invented in Persia, and the Persian understands better than anyone the disillusioned fatalism of this quatrain of Omar Khayyám. He too is indifferent to the "two days" sung by the poet: "unborn tomorrow and dead yesterday."

Hence that duality which, with the Persian more than any other mortal, lies at the base of the national character: in his heart of hearts, an ardent spirituality and almost morbid sensibility; outwardly, a detachment and skepticism verging on cynicism. Within, a mystic; without, a mystifier.

Is it any wonder then that the behavior of the average Persian so often takes a theatrical turn, toward comedy or tragedy, as the case may be? No other explanation can account for the passion of the masses for Dr. Mohammed Mossadegh. Sobbing distractedly at the mere thought of the country's misfortunes, jeering at the foreigner, defying the powers-that-be, and adroitly mixing fable and reality, the "old fox" thrilled and delighted the little people of Iran. He was Punchinello and Karaguez rolled into one.

By dint of overacting the part, one gets swept away by the melodrama of it all. The hysterical bigots who still today, when the day of "Ashura" comes around, run wild in the streets of Iranian cities, punctuating with sobs and lamentations the blows and mutilations they inflict on themselves, do more than commemorate the tragic death of Imam Hosain: *they re-experience it.*

Under a beautiful starry sky, one night a short time ago in a small village near Rizaiyeh, a traveling cinema set up its screen in the open air and projected a Western. When the villain carried off the heroine on his prancing horse, all the men in the audience made a dash for their own mounts and without further ado galloped off in pursuit of the kidnaper.

Another day, at Tehran, a few sorry-looking smugglers were being judged. A trial, more than any other event of daily life, is first and foremost a piece of public entertainment. The families of the accused come flocking in as if they were attending a theater. It so happened in this instance that the courtroom was too small to hold all these good people. The police, though raining blows with their heavy sticks, had all they could do to hold back the crowd, who redoubled their piteous outcries and appeals in hopes of softening the hearts of the guards. From the dock the accused lifted up their voices in indignant lamentation: their relatives and friends were being deprived of a performance to which they were entitled. The public felt the injustice of it and took their part. Voices rose in pitch. Sobbing and groaning broke out on all sides. The emotional excitement spread to the bench, playing on the feelings of judges, clerks, and even prison guards. Finally, in the general uproar, the defending lawyers had no trouble in securing a verdict of not guilty.

All this is apt to baffle a foreigner. As far as he can see, this overwrought emotionalism is mere hypocrisy or childishness. If he ever finds himself the target of it, he will angrily put it down to xenophobia. But the truth lies elsewhere, and things—especially in Persia—are not what they seem. Iranians are ceaselessly weighing and comparing. It is difficult to take in a people whose daily life draws at every moment on the lessons of five thousand years. A century or so ago the European commanded respect and esteem all over Asia. Amidst the general corruption and cruelty he alone appeared honest, courageous, human— in a word, superior. Little by little Westerners have worn off that luster. They, like everyone else, have been found alive to the lure of fat profits, cleverer perhaps in corrupting others, but more vulnerable when corrupt themselves. The bubble got pricked, and the myth of the West vanished into thin air.

The Persian is proud. He is quite capable of despising a newcomer if he thinks he can dominate him, beguile him, deflate him, and then elude him if need be. The Persian is boastful, yet prompt to detect boasting in others and to expose it ruthlessly.

A rose was saying: I am the wonder of the world.
Turn, and hide, and smile.

The critical moment comes when, smiling to himself, your Persian creases his heavy eyelids and undertakes to get the better of you. But let him know he has a friend before him, let him raise his eyelids, and then a sudden change occurs: the truth dawns on him and a human contact is made. From a rather dim, elusive individual, deliberately out to browbeat the foreigner, he becomes a subtle, sensitive, courageous observer, ready to take a new friend to his bosom and enlighten him as to the hitherto puzzling ways of a strange country.

And for the country too the same change occurs. Step out of your foreigner's shoes, come halfway and a little more, make friends and entertain; all Persia will take on a new look. At the end of sordid lanes, doors open and make way for you. The wonderful gardens you thought existed only in legends rise before your eyes, with their fragrant profusion of plant life, their pools and aviaries. Families welcome you into their midst, with their laughter-loving women, delightful creatures, unburdened by any of the complexes of their Moslem sisters.

Without standing on ceremony they will invite you to those dainty Persian meals which come as such a welcome change after the insipid menus *à la française* served today in all the hotels on the globe. Then begins your initiation into the thousand and one ways of preparing rice; then begins your experience of herbs, sauces, and scents that will prove to you what a privileged few know already: that Persian cooking can vie with the best in the world. The humblest home will welcome you with hearty hospitality around the traditional *coursi,* the poor man's stove, whose comforting warmth finds no escape amid the rugs and furs that surround you.

What only yesterday had struck you as inexplicable indifference has now come to look very much like wisdom: "You know you have no power over your destiny," writes the Persian poet, "you know not whence you come, you know not whither you go: why does the uncertainty of the morrow cause you any anxiety?" The politeness—you thought it was overdone—with which the Persians greet you, and anxiously inquire into the state of your affairs and your health, no longer seems obsequious; since everyone indulges in the ceremony and no one attaches any particular intention to it, may it not be after all an excellent means of smoothing the relations between people of one and the same society, and no more overdone than the set phrases of compliment and salutation with which Europeans end their letters?

And above all, once initiated, the foreigner will discover what life means to a Persian, what it has and holds for him. The quest of honors and riches preoccupies him less, as a rule, than the answer he seeks to his personal problems.

> *A little bread, a little water,*
> *Your eyes, the shade, the morn.*
> *No sultan could be happier,*
> *No beggar more forlorn....*

However happy he may be, the Persian will always experience an undertaste of bitterness in things. Of the vanity of the world he is well aware; he is the first to poke fun, among intimates, at the glories he takes pleasure in parading before the foreigner. "Our civilization is fifty-seven years older than the five thousand ascribed to it," a Persian diplomat told us one day.

"Why so?"

"Because I've been hearing about it now for fifty-seven years!"

For the people who have been called the "Frenchmen of the East" have—as you will find out for yourself once you get to know them—a sense of humor which admits very largely of self-mockery. The Englishman James Morier and the Frenchman Gobineau have amusingly described the foibles and oddities of their Persian hosts. Both these authors are highly esteemed in Persia. But let anyone else venture a joke at their expense, even the most harmless pleasantry, and Iran will never forgive him.

Such is roughly the picture of this alluring country, where suffering and death are inseparably coupled with the sweetness of life, where poets either are venerated or kill themselves, where the sadness of the people shows through at every moment beneath their insouciance. "Hapless chicken," says the Persian proverb, "whether funeral or wedding, it gets its head cut off."

A country as old as the world, but growing younger every day. A country where the certainty of survival is unshakable. When you have subdued the conquering Greek, triumphed over the power of Rome, assimilated the Arab invader, held out against the Mongol, contained the Ottoman empire, and—unique in contemporary annals—loosened the iron grip of the Red Army on a province all but lost, then what have you to fear of the future? The best argument in favor of the continued existence of this country is that it has been able to survive up to now.

No wonder that with the divine Hafiz of Shiraz, the greatest lyric poet of Persia and no doubt of the whole Middle East, Persians keep their faith in the coming of better days:

Joseph lost will find his way to the land of Canaan
Be not sad

The humble house of sorrow will become a garden
Be not sad

O aching heart, all will mend
Do not despair, your restless thoughts
Subsiding, in peace will end
Be not sad

If another spring of life is born
Song bird, come you must once more
Within the shady tent of flowers
Above the throne of grasslands
Be not sad

If two days long desire goes unsatisfied
Although the spinning world spins on

Tell yourself the motion of the earth
Is never the same

                    Be not sad

When you strike into the desert
Pilgrim-hearted, full of faith
If the bushes skin your feet

                    Be not sad

Though night is nigh and shelter uncertain
And your destination still remote
Know for certain
Every journey has its end

                    Be not sad.

In Azerbaijan, at Tabriz, from the tower of the ark, or citadel, with its vestiges of ancient Persia, the traveler has, spread before him, a symbolic picture of present-day Iran. The gaze drops down to the Mosque of Saheb-eh Amr, glowing white at the foot of purple mountains, its minarets sparkling in the sun. This is the mosque of the "Master of Time," of the Messiah, of Him who is to come. From the humblest to the highest, all alike in Persia await the coming of the Master of Time, who will reduce the cost of living, ward off the threat of foreign invasion, prevent the landlord from squeezing the peasant and the politician from confusing the people's well-being with his own.

Son and heir of eternal Persia, Iran is slowly waking up to the realities of modern life, and may be expected to take its rightful place in the modern world. It is a country which will never meet with indifference: either you take to it passionately or you hate it.

Chapter One

3

Uplands

1 From the foot of Mount Ararat to the plains of Khurasan, the Elburz raises its mighty mountain wall across the north of Iran. Its highest peak, Mount Demavend (18,600 feet), is an extinct volcano, now keeping quiet vigil over Tehran.

The southern slope, facing the desert, is inhabited by shepherd folk and herdsmen whose dwellings form two distinct settlements: *bala-bala,* the upper town, and *payin-payin,* the lower town.

Shown here is a *bala-bala* with its primitive, mud-walled hovels and their characteristic terraced roofs. The latter are built on *hassir,* matting stretched between logs and covered with beaten earth. The cattle are kept within the garth or enclosure in daytime, then herded into dugout cellars at nightfall.

In the foreground is the *kalamestan* or poplar nursery. With the sale of these trees the mountaineer ekes out the meager income he earns from stock-farming. The *tabrizi* (poplar) offers the double advantage of growing fast and growing straight, which thus spares the trouble of squaring the timber.

The Elburz

2 Fifty thousand years ago, at the end of the Paleolithic Age, the Caspian, together with the Aral and the mouths of the great rivers of Central Asia, formed an immense inland sea. The southernmost expanse of its waters covered a large part of Iran. A vestige of it remains in the Shureh, a vast area of swampland and salt marshes.

One of the labors performed by Rustam, the legendary hero, consisted in slaying the Divehsefid, a white monster, half man, half tiger, which lived in a cave in the Elburz. With his bare hands the hero dug the ground out from under the sleeping dragon and, lifting it bodily into the air, dashed it against the rocks. The *Shahnama,* which relates Rustam's exploits, describes him as capable of outracing wild asses and, when hungry, of capturing two or three in less time than it takes to tell, spitting them on trees which he uprooted for that purpose, and roasting them whole.

Even today the virgin forests of the Elburz still abound in tigers, panthers, bears, and deer.

Resht

3 The wall of the Elburz range is left behind. The mountain streams rushing down its northern slopes

melt away in the swamps before reaching the Caspian Sea. Here water is the dominant element: rice paddies follow the tea plantations introduced by the former Prime Minister Ghavam Saltaneh. Houses have to be built on piles; the terraced roofs found everywhere else in Persia give way now to high-pitched thatched roofs, the only ones that keep out the rain. This region is an angler's paradise; here he can choose between the sweet-water streams, teeming with salmon and trout, and the salt waters of the Caspian, full of sturgeon.

Then, as we go north, Resht suddenly comes into sight, one of the most recently built, most pleasant towns in the country. To be "recently built" in Iran means not to go back any further than the fourteenth century. And a smiling, gracious place it is with its lush gardens and well-tilled fields, its thriving silk industry, and its spirited girls. Alluvial deposits form a golden belt around Resht, richly planted with vineyards and olive groves, orange trees and sugar cane, tobacco and cotton.

Pahlevi

4 The reigning dynasty has given its name to the main Persian port on the Caspian, where it won its first victory. It was here in 1920 that Bolshevik troops landed to prevent Persia from falling under British domination. When Riza Pahlevi contrived to make both of them evacuate Persian territory, his name was taken, as a token of gratitude, by the town of Enzeli, whose location makes it a kind of sentinel at the northern tip of the country, facing the incalculable Slav.

For a long time the town controlled one of the two routes leading into Persia: the route from Russia through Baku. The other, across the deserts of Syria and Iraq, has been practicable only since the French mandate in the Levant, which for the first time guaranteed the security of travelers.

Pahlevi represents, first of all, caviar. The sturgeon of the Caspian go up the Volga for breeding purposes and then spawn along the Iranian coast. These curious migratory habits, unknown to the ancients, greatly intrigued Marco Polo. "From the first day of Lent to Holy Saturday, on Easter eve, fish aplenty are to be found, and the finest in the world," he wrote. "But at all other times of the year, not a fish is to be found until Lent comes round again; so it goes, year in, year out, a pure miracle."

Russians and Iranians long collaborated in supplying the world with caviar: the Pahlevi fishing stations were a Russian concession and Russians attended to the business of selling the fish and its precious roe, and to the equally important duty of periodically restocking the Caspian Sea. But this arrangement fell a victim to the oil war: to counterbalance the nationalization of Abadan in the south, in 1951, the Mossadegh government in the same year abrogated the fishing concessions in the north. So now the Iranians alone produce caviar at Pahlevi, but the yield is growing smaller each year; the Russians have built hydroelectric dams on the Volga, and the sturgeon, for reasons known only to themselves, refuse to go through the special floodgates installed to enable them to ascend the river.

Ramsar

5 European peasants in the Middle Ages were dressed in just this way: tunics and breeches of coarse wool, soft felt shoes secured with leather straps. On top of this, a sleeveless sheepskin cape with the woolly side innermost, warm against the body. A bonnet of lamb's wool and mufflers complete the outfit necessary to bear up under wind, cold, and rain or perpetual damp.

This is the home of astrakhan, the soft fur of a lamb torn from the womb of the ewe before the end of her pregnancy. This region, with its pastoral economy, where men's needs are few, is absolutely self-sufficing. Sheep and goats supply the inhabitants with clothes and food. Money hereabouts is practically unknown; the produce of the livestock serves to pay in kind for the rent of the poor pasture land and to barter for indispensable articles. The inhabitants build their own houses—mere wooden shanties, without a nail in them, held together by thongs and pegs.

In the distance rise the majestic buildings of Ramsar and Babolsar, summer resorts on the shore of the Caspian, where the authorities are trying to establish a Persian Riviera.

Chapter Two

6 *And the thirteenth day everyone is out of doors . . .*

For the Persians the year begins in the spring. The season of budding life, fresh colors, and unsophisticated joys also inaugurates the fiscal year. Unlike the other Moslem peoples, whose months are fixed by the phases of the moon, Iranians have always kept to the solar year of the old Sassanian calendar. *Now Rooz,* the Persian New Year, is celebrated on March 21. But the great holiday is *sisdeh,* the thirteenth day after *Now Rooz,* when the whole population indulges in public rejoicing.

Sisdeh bedar, chaharda betu, "the thirteenth outside, the fourteenth at home," runs a popular saying in Persia. Superstition has it that to spend either a *sisdeh* indoors or a *chaharda* out brings bad luck.

So dressed in their Sunday best, with heaped-up food baskets and plenty of rugs in a cart or loaded on a mule, each family wends its way out of the city on that day, to obviate any risk of drawing evil influences down on their heads.

Across the length and breadth of the land an immense picnic is spread on the grass—or the ground, where no grass grows. Millions of samovars pour out fragrant cups of tea; the wealthy bring along their musicians, the poor their gramophones. Platters full of sherbets, pistachios, watermelon seeds, and a thousand other delicacies pass from hand to hand. Whole lambs equally roast to a turn on skewers over wood fires in the open, and then are served with rice in a delicious *chelo kebab.*

Children play at *asyab chereh* (cartwheels) till they fall over from sheer dizziness.

The men play backgammon, or chat and argue, drawing the while on their *kalians* and puffing clouds of smoke into the air. Young couples sing to themselves, soft and low, a choice quatrain or two of Omar Khayyám:

> *Come, fill the Cup, and in the fire of Spring*
> *Your Winter-garment of Repentance fling:*
> *The Bird of Time has but a little way*
> *To flutter—and the Bird is on the Wing.*

Girls tie two blades of grass crosswise and make the wish to find a husband in the coming year; married women wish for children.

The same day, the *sabzehs* are thrown into rivers and streams all over the country; these are green plants which, grown for this particular purpose well before the *Now Rooz,* begin to wither on the thirteenth day.

At nightfall, filled with hopes of better things in a new year so joyfully begun, and mindful of the proverb which says "the year depends on its springtime," everyone prepares to spend the next day under his own roof: *chaharda betu,* the fourteenth at home.

If it die . . .

7 On the southern outskirts of Tehran the rich clay soil is soft and pliable. Kilns have been established there to fire the bricks that will go to build cities. But the prospective buyer trembles at the sight of the bricks, the workmen themselves go reluctantly about their tasks.

Only a few years ago this area was given over to cemeteries. In accordance with Moslem tradition, the dead are buried coffinless, merely wrapped in the shroud they have worn all their life as turban or veil. Their bodies have turned into clay. These *ajoreh ablar* (red bricks) and *resht* (dried bricks) are thus a literal illustration of Omar Khayyám's verses:

> *Surely not in vain*
> *My substance of the common Earth was ta'en*
> *And to this Figure moulded, to be broke,*
> *Or trampled back to shapeless Earth again.*

Today these cemeteries lie within walled enclosures. And the brick-making zone is the haunt of vagrants, opium addicts, and the down-and-out; in dugouts and hovels hereabouts live poverty-stricken families with no other home to call their own.

But in Iran high life and low life are never very far apart. Close by is the little town of Rai, built on the vestiges of a city that goes back perhaps as far as 3000 B.C., the ancient Raghae. Alexander the Great stopped here. The Seleucid emperors embellished the place and called it Europus. It was the residence of the Caliph El Mansur, the founder of Baghdad. It was the birthplace of Harun al-Rashid, celebrated in the *Thousand and One Nights.* Rai marked the terminus of the Silk Route, over which, of old, countless caravans pursued the even tenor of their way, laden with eastern treasure, fabrics, dainties, spices.

The Iranian is well aware of this, and when he looks at the humble, rather tawdry modern town molded in the clay of the ancient metropolis, he feels obscurely that man too is vulnerable, frail and transient as baked clay, and he understands the prayer, overheard by the poet, which it murmurs:

> *For I remember stopping by the way*
> *To watch a Potter thumping his wet Clay:*
> *And with its all-obliterated Tongue*
> *It murmured—"Gently, Brother, gently, pray!"*

For the love of God

8 "The merchant: one who fears not God." This definition, coined in the fourteenth century by the satirical poet Obaid Zakani, no doubt fails to apply to the shopkeeper of Isfahan whose wares are displayed here. For beside his crates of onions, strings of *khorma kharak* (green dates), and barrel of oil to keep the lamps of the neighborhood burning, this honest tradesman has set up a *sakkahaneh,* that "Wallace fountain" of Iranian Islam.

The Shiite doctrine professed by Iranian Islam in defiance of the Sunnite orthodoxy is based on respect for the Imams, successors of the Prophet Mohammed through his grandson Hosain. The latter—whose wife was a Persian princess, daughter of the Sassanian Prince Yazdegher—was done to death in the desert of Mesopotamia by his rival Yazid, who overcame the resistance of Hosain and his followers only by cutting off their water supply.

In memory of Hosain's martyrdom, pious Iranians endow charitable societies whose object is to distribute water gratis to the needy; hence the *sakkahanehs.* These as a rule are sheet-metal tanks shaped like Hosain's tomb and decorated with scenes of the saint's life and death. Sometimes they are embellished with gold and silver ex-votos, on which pious hands place lighted candles.

It so happens, moreover, that Iranian grocers are usually *hadji, kerbelai,* or *meshedis*—pilgrims, that is, who have paid the ritual visit to the holy places at Mecca, Kerbela, or Meshed. Added to the fact that he is usually pretty well off, this distinction, signalized by the wearing of a gold-colored turban, makes the grocer a man of consequence.

To his clientele he dispenses every item conceivably necessary to the business of housekeeping, from spices and the usual foodstuffs to *mast* (yoghurt), tobacco, and candles. He opens his shop at daybreak and keeps it open till midnight. In districts where electricity is unknown, his house is the only one always lighted, like a beacon. When the nocturnal wayfarer glimpses the grocer's lights, his heart is cheered.

Chapter Three

9

14

Isfahan

9 A garden, roses trembling in the breeze, cypress trees, red lips and heady wine, a nightingale singing to a rose—something like this is the image evoked the world over by the magic word Isfahan.

To make his capital seem indeed *nesfeh jahan,* "one half of the world," Shah Abbas created wonders and sowed the place thick with palaces, caravanserais, mosques, and colleges. "It must be acknowledged," wrote Gobineau in the nineteenth century, "that its immense edifices, painted, gilded, enameled as they are, its blue or flower-patterned walls reflecting the rays of the sun, its vast bazaars and extensive gardens, its plane trees and roses make Isfahan the paragon of elegance and the acme of prettiness."

Here is the back of the decor, a glimpse behind the scenes. No city is beautiful or celebrated in the East unless, in the eyes of the bedazzled traveler overcome by the desert heat and the desert sands, it looms up before him in the shape of an oasis. The secret of Isfahan, of Damascus and Samarkand too, is water.

Shah Abbas swelled the river watering the town, at great expense, Sir John Chardin tells us, by cutting through the mountains thirty leagues distant from Isfahan. Tapped all along its course, the river irrigates gardens and grounds through numberless furrows and channels. Its waters keep the city clean, for all the house drains end in the street and serve as washing places in the poorer districts. The veil worn by these washerwomen is not a religious accessory. The Moslem woman uses it as a shield: against prying eyes, especially if she is young and pretty, and against the burning heat of the sun, for the swarthy, olive-skinned Oriental sets great store by a wife with a pink and white complexion. And above all, the veil is a convenient covering, masking the shabbiness of the clothes beneath or simply dispensing a woman from dressing up every time she goes out.

The birth of a marvel

10 If you have ever let your fancy roam before the enchantments of a Persian rug, take a close look at this *khan* in the bazaar of Isfahan. In these squalid surroundings a work of art is created. This is the *rangrazi,* the open-air laboratory where marvelous colors are born.

As they come from the dyer's, the skeins of wool are laid out on logs to dry in the sun. Heating in the great brick kiln, the *tanur,* are vegetable colors whose recipe is a family secret, jealously kept and handed down from father to son.

Rug and tapestry making is a popular art in Iran. In the remotest villages the women spend the long winter evenings weaving *kilims* or lock-stitching rugs on rudimentary looms. The patterns come directly from everyday life: flowers, fruit, vegetables, wild and domestic animals, alternating with stylized arabesques. Colors vary from region to region, blue predominating in the north, purple in the south.

The dye works in the bazaar also dress the linen *karvan* which serves to make that indispensable accessory of every Moslem: his shroud.

Smoke

11 A purveyor of delicate sensations is the kalian dealer. He makes his pipes out of the wood of wild cherry trees; but only the wild cherry of Luristan and Bakhtiari will do, and he prefers to go and fetch it himself on long expeditions made periodically.

The kalian fits onto a flask of fresh, scented water through which the smoke passes before being inhaled through a wooden stem. And the blissful smoker proceeds to forget his cares and indulge in happy pipe dreams.

For Persians, as they sit cross-legged on upholstered benches with a glass of fragrant, syrupy tea beside them, the kalian hour is the best hour of the day.

> *Ah, my Belovéd, fill the cup that clears*
> To-DAY *of past Regrets and future Fears:*
> *To-morrow!—Why, To-morrow I may be*
> *Myself with Yesterday's Sev'n thousand Years....*
>
> *Ah, make the most of what we yet may spend,*
> *Before we too into the Dust descend....*

Gold and silver

12 Like carpet weavers, the gold- and silversmiths decorate their wares not only with geometric designs but also with the age-old themes of Persian legend and history. Each town has themes and patterns peculiarly its own; common to all, however, are the eggplant and above all the cypress, which, in a manner of speaking, is the trademark of Iran. But the chased silver of Isfahan and Shiraz is the most famous of all.

Displayed here on the shelves of a shop is fine silverware which will soon add luster to the home of some well-to-do Persian: kalian and samovar, pitcher and ewer, platters and tea-glass holders.

The metal is first hammered so fine that it has to be laid out on wax and worked with a needle. Each hole is then blacked with a pen. So delicate is the best work that it requires the very finest fingers. Barefoot, working the belt of a primitive lathe with his knee, and already a skilled craftsman in spite of his age, this boy hardly imagines that his handiwork will carry the fame of Persian art and culture to the ends of the earth.

Shiraz, heaven and hell

13
> *A garden, a lissome girl,*
> *A jug of wine:*
> *My heartsease, my heartache,*
> *My Heaven-Hell.*

Life seems good in Shiraz, with its smiling daughters and good-humored sons. Yet Gobineau hated the place, which harbors, according to him, "the greatest rogues in the Empire, who have the insolence of a Paris streetboy and his delight in evil-doing." However this may be, the city itself is one of the loveliest in the East.

Like Persia itself, Shiraz has been overrun more than once, bending to the conqueror's yoke, then lifting up its head with a smile when better times returned. A flourishing metropolis in the twelfth century, it was razed by Tamerlane; thriving again in the fifteenth century, it was ravaged by flood waters in 1688 and sacked by the Afghans thirty years later.

Thanks to the "regent" Karim, who made it the capital of Persia in the mid-eighteenth century under the Zond Dynasty, and embellished it with palaces, *medressehs,* and fine brick buildings, all overtopped by the onion-shaped cupolas of the Fars mosques, Shiraz today is again coquettish and carefree, with its mild climate, its busy bazaars and handicrafts—and the prettiest girls in Persia, hymned by Saadi and Hafiz.

After leaving Isfahan and crossing a monotonous stretch of country, the overland traveler abruptly enters a narrow gorge and then, in the midst of a natural amphitheater, in a lush and sunny valley, gets his first sight of the "city of poets." For such is the name it goes by—much to be envied in a country where the "princes of poetry" had their mouths filled with gold pieces in gratitude for their poems.

The town is surrounded by gardens where still today attar of rose is distilled. Each tiny bottle of it represents the essence of a ton of rose petals. There are market gardens and orchards lovingly cultivated; cucumbers and lemons, pears and cherries, green almonds and grapes; grapes in abundance; the famous *khollar gwei,* whose juice intoxicated Roman emperors.

The vine and that yellow, wine-filled cup called the sun are the theme song of Persian poetry.

> *And lately, by the Tavern Door agape,*
> *Came shining through the Dusk an Angel Shape*
> *Bearing a Vessel on his Shoulder; and*
> *He bid me taste of it; and 'twas—the Grape!*

> *The Grape that can with Logic absolute*
> *The Two-and-Seventy jarring Sects confute:*
> *The sovereign Alchemist that in a trice*
> *Life's leaden metal into Gold transmute.*

The Epicurean exultation of Omar Khayyám answers the exhortations of Firdousi:

> *The coward drinks it, and grows a hero,*
> *The wretch drinks deep, and grows glad,*
> *And his cheeks glow like the pomegranate blossom.*

A hundred years ago when Pasteur called wine the "milk of grown-ups," he little thought that a Persian poet had forged the same image eight centuries before:

> *As the child needs milk, so the man needs wine.*
> *Let the dawn-awakened cock crow,*
> *Then tune your lyre with him*
> *And quench your thirst.*

At the bazaar of Yezd: the tinker

14 Like most Persian towns, Yezd is an oasis. It lies in the heart of Iran, lost in the immense central desert whose desolate salt flats daunted even the Mongols. The whole interior of the Iranian plateau is desert waste, from the Elburz in the north to Makran in the south, from the Zagros in the west to the Afghan frontier on the east.

Yezd lies well off the great highroads, and therefore suffered little from the great invasions. Marco Polo went out of his way to visit it, and Tamerlane to capture it.

It used to be a thriving town, a main stopping place on the Silk Route. Today its hard-working craftsmen are the only visible sign of activity.

The isolation of the place no doubt accounts for the survival of the Zoroastrian community. Yezd in fact is one of the most important centers of the Zoroastrian religion. The Ghebers, fire worshipers who have preserved their Mazdaist beliefs in the teeth of all Islam, were all-powerful under the Sassanian kings two thousand years ago. The sect numbers a bare twenty thousand today, about a third of whom live in a compact community at Yezd. Hence the "towers of silence," at a short distance from the town, on which the Zoroastrian dead are ritually exposed to carrion-eating birds, in order that none of the elements may be sullied by their bodies.

By their headdress shall you know them. In Persia, and all over the East, headgear is almost always a sure indication of social status, race, and religion. The tinsmith on the left is a Gheber: the form of his turban vouches for it. The cobbler on the right is a Moslem: witness the *arakchin,* or embroidered cap, on his shaven head.

The operation of re-tinning requires careful preparation. Before a fresh coat of tin can be applied, the objects must be cleaned, as follows. First they are plunged into a tub of wet sand. Then the craftsman takes hold of a ring fastened to the ceiling overhead, and swinging from this he pushes them about in the sand with his bare feet in an extraordinary kind of "hula," setting the rhythm himself with a Parsee chant.

The cobbler

15 At Yezd everybody seems to go slipshod, and the cobbler has his work cut out for him. To produce the rough sandals required by his clientele, he begins by a round of rag-picking: any rag, tatter, or shred of cloth will do. These he washes, dyes blue, and presses flat, like so many pancakes. A half-dozen thicknesses suffice for the sole; a sliver of leather reinforces each end, while with their white hands young girls of the town weave the vamp in gay colors. The result is a pair of *givehs* or Persian sandals.

All shapes and colors of wood

16 Midway between carpentry and marquetry comes Persian *haratti.* All wood and nothing but wood,

from the *duk* (spinning wheel) to the *gushkoos* (pestle). To the *haratti* man the baby owes his toys and his first steps in a play pen, the girl her combs, and the old woman her bobbins.

Fruit and spices at Isfahan

17 Having thrown two red bath towels over his bare body, the *dalak* drops in at the grocer's. The *dalak* is the masseur at the Turkish baths next door: a go-between, insinuates Obaid Zakani in a famous Persian poem. He fills an important function in Oriental society, where the public baths are an indispensable feature of daily life; people resort to them constantly in order to keep their weight down, in a country where rich foods and sweets are rather the rule than the exception. Yet Iranians on the whole tend to be thin—except the gymnasts, strange as it may seem.

The food business in Persia, as everywhere else, is highly profitable. The Spice Route, like the Gold and Silk Routes, has attracted many a shrewd and ambitious businessman. Here is a fine choice of spices and foods for sale in the bazaar of Isfahan: aromatics and condiments, saffron and cloves, grain and seeds, rice and dried vegetables, pistachio nuts and apricot paste, in addition to strings of *limu omani,* tiny Shiraz lemons used only when dried and shriveled up.

This lavish display is obviously that of a well-to-do tradesman. Clean-shaven (by means of a pair of clippers, for Shiite Moslems object to razor blades) and sporting a white shirt with a detachable collar (which he has detached), the height of elegance for a Persian market, the *baghal* has multiplied the tokens of his prosperity: mirrors on every wall, oil lamps, Isfahan vases, and above all, hanging from the ceil-ing, those many-colored glass balls which passing children long to lay their hands on.

The bazaar plays an important part in the life of the country. Concentrated here, and grouped in trade guilds, are the shopkeepers and craftsmen who form the "third estate" in Persia. On the bazaar, which masses the bulk of producers in the heart of each urban area, depends the life of the city. Whenever the bazaar closes down, all activity ceases and the town takes on an air of faintly sinister expectation, as if trouble were brewing.

One of the pillars of law and order, always respectful of authority, but indignant at bribery and corruption, cramped by age-old privileges of birth, oppressed by the great landowners, the bazaar has played a key part in every revolutionary movement. It was only because he had the bazaar behind him that Dr. Mossadegh, hero of the nationalization of the oil wells, came to power in 1951. On the bazaar today depends the success of the modernization program undertaken by the Shah.

Here are employment and productive money. Here the fluctuations of the dollar and the price of gold can be watched, and the power of the hour instantly recognized. Before the war the bazaar was fiercely pro-German. Germany at that time accounted for forty-eight per cent of Persia's export trade and seemed to constitute a third force between England and Russia.

For years after the war the odds were in favor of the United States. The Americans' currency was hard, the economic plans sponsored by them were good for business, and tended toward a certain social equality. But for some time now the bazaar has been pricking up its ears at certain rumors from the rest of the Moslem world, which have it that the Russians . . .

Chapter Four

18 In comparison with the five thousand years Persian civilization can boast of, Tehran cuts the figure of an adolescent; it was still a village seven centuries ago and has been the capital for only a hundred and sixty years.

The founder of the Kajar Dynasty, Agha Mohammed, made Tehran the seat of the Empire. Agha Mohammed's life was dedicated to revenge. His father, Khan, stemming from a Tartar tribe of the Caspian region, was deposed by Nadir Shah in 1737. The latter, to make assurance doubly sure, carried off Agha Mohammed as a hostage and had him castrated at Meshed. When he reached manhood, the eunuch prince contrived his escape and methodically undertook the conquest of the Empire. This he achieved in 1787 and, abandoning Shiraz and Meshed, the capitals of his predecessors, he established his throne at Tehran. His family—which descended from his nephew Fath Ali Shah—reigned until 1923, when Riza Shah, father of the present sovereign, proclaimed himself emperor.

Under both dynasties Tehran was embellished and enriched with numerous monuments, and though it cannot vie in beauty with Isfahan or Shiraz, it has gradually taken on the air of a metropolis. Its broad avenues, its sheltered gardens, and huge buildings, put up by Riza Shah, make it a thoroughly modern city, growing with a steady influx of new inhabitants from all over Persia.

The Golestan, the palace of the Rose Garden, remains its most sumptuous monument. There, in the immense, honeycombed room that forms the heart of the building, stand the presents offered to Iranian sovereigns or the booty brought back from their campaigns. The set of Sèvres porcelain offered by Napoleon stands beside magnificent cameos, armor, gold plate, vases of jade. There glitters the famous Peacock Throne, set with countless precious stones, which serves for the coronation of the Shah-in-Shah.

At the Golestan the sovereigns hold their *salam,* receptions of government and diplomatic officials on the occasion of the New Year. On that day, as in all Persian homes, the palace is transformed for the *Now Rooz.* To begin with, on a table lavishly decorated and decked with flowers, the *haft sin* are placed, "seven objects" whose Persian names begin with "s": *sabzeh,* greens, *samak,* a spice used to flavor the pilaff, *sombol,* narcissus, *serkeh,* vinegar, *sanjed,* sesame, *sib,* apples, *sir,* fresh garlic. It does not matter what the objects are, provided there are seven of them and their names begin with the fateful letter.

In Moslem Persia, Zoroastrian magic is still very much alive. The country that adopted the Koranic faith of its Arabian invaders has still not forgotten the rites its ancestors were practicing five thousand years ago—the religion of the Magi, of sun and fire.

Salam *at the Golestan*

_{19/20} The viziers, or high dignitaries, have all turned out in court dress, befitting the occasion: Salam day at the Golestan. All state bodies attend and present their respects to the sovereigns on New Year's Day. With a brisk step, wearing the uniform of Marshal of the Imperial Forces, His Majesty Mohammed Riza Pahlevi, Shah-in-Shah, King of Kings, makes his entrance.

The astrakhan toque, the interminable tuft on an ostrich-egg diamond, the scimitars and medals, the pearls, and emeralds, are no more than memories of a bygone age.

Mohammed Riza Shah is a modern ruler. Dark, slender-hipped, broad-shouldered, wavy-haired, sharp-eyed, with a hint of sadness in his glance, he is a keen sportsman, and the more strenuous the sport, the better he likes it. He is hard to beat at chess and polo, which is as it should be, for both of these games were invented in Persia. He pilots his own plane, a B-17, and makes frequent hops to every corner of his empire. He is as much steeped in French culture as he is in Persian philosophy, and speaks English fluently. The dominant trait of his character is mysticism, a kind of pantheism embracing all the religions that have gained a following in Persia, from Zoroaster to Islam and all its schisms. In every event of daily life the Shah sees a manifestation of the spirits of good or evil. It is this inner force, he told us one day, that dictated his decision to distribute the crown lands among the landless peasants.

This was the young prince who, in 1941, was called on to succeed his father Riza Pahlevi, whom the united forces of the Soviet Union and Great Britain had driven from the Persian throne, and who was to die in an English detention camp.

The personality of Riza Pahlevi dominates the whole history of Iran in our time. He was born in Mazandaran, a province of greatly mixed population, owing to successive invasions, and he must have been of Kurd or Turkish extraction, like all the leaders of men who have dominated Persia. He began his career as a plain soldier in the brigade of Persian Cossacks formed and led by Russians, and he rose rapidly in rank. His military prowess, his commanding figure, and his mettlesome energy attracted the attention of the British who, in 1920, put him in command of the local troops raised to resist the landing of Bolshevik forces at Enzeli. In February 1921 he turned on Tehran, took it without firing a shot, and set up a new government in which he allotted himself the key post of war minister. He then mapped out a vast program of national recovery, of which the first step was to re-establish Persian independence. The new master of Tehran first concluded a treaty with the Russians, in terms of which all previous pacts were canceled and the Soviet Union formally renounced the zone of influence which the Czars had so jealously guarded in Iran. Then, on the strength of this success, Riza denounced the protectorate agreement imposed on Iran by Great Britain in 1919.

Having rid himself of the tutelage (and interference) of the two great powers that had split the country between them, Riza deposed the Kajar Dynasty, proclaimed himself Shah in 1925, and undertook to break the influence of the tribal chiefs by subjecting them to the authority of the central government.

Riza Pahlevi reduced the privileges enjoyed by foreign powers, abolished the old treaties of extraterritoriality, weaned the people from archaic customs imposed by tradition and fanaticism, forbade the wearing of veils, suppressed titles of nobility, created industries almost out of nothing, developed agriculture, reduced illiteracy, built the great Trans-Iranian. In a word, he forged modern Iran.

Skillfully playing off one power against the other, the new emperor succeeded in making himself feared and respected. Nothing shows this more clearly than the way the envoys of the Western powers and those of Hitler, Mussolini, and Stalin vied with each other in currying favor with him in the thirties. Everything served as a pretext to assert and consolidate his authority. Just before the war an innocent joke in a Paris weekly so much offended the Shah that he broke off diplomatic relations with France. It took no less than a full-dress military mission headed by General Maxime Weygand, sent out to Iran in 1939 for the marriage of the Shah's son, to repair the damage to Franco-Iranian relations.

This, in brief, was the achievement of the man who, in September 1941, was forced to abdicate by the British and Soviet authorities. Iran at the time was teeming with Axis agents who, under cover of commercial and industrial transactions, were actually carrying on espionage and sabotage on a scale that seriously threatened Allied security, at a time when Russia had to be helped at all costs, and when German troops were sweeping over Libya, Greece, and the Caucasus.

In the early years of Mohammed Riza's reign, Iran enjoyed hardly a moment of peace and security. Until the end of the Second World War the Allies governed the country, and their decisions were law. After succeeding to the throne in 1941, the young ruler was not even certain what the Russians and British intended him to do, or intended to do with him. Then, when the war was over, trouble broke out in Azerbaijan. Cut off from the rest of Persia by Soviet occupation, the great northern province launched a secession movement under the impetus of the Azeri democratic party. Kurdistan in turn proclaimed itself an independent republic. Even in Tehran the pro-communist Tudeh party widened its influence and dominated the government. Finally the Red Army agreed to evacuate its occupation zone, exacting in exchange the promise that an oil concession in the north would be granted to Russia.

At this critical juncture the young ruler showed for the first time an energy and courage which took everyone by surprise. Gradually the Tehran government managed to eliminate communist influence in Azerbaijan, then in the rest of Iran. The Persian leaders displayed in fact a keen insight into the Russian mind and cleverly foresaw what the Stalinist reaction would be. They contrived to confront the Soviet Union with the following dilemma: either to support the communists at all costs in Azerbaijan, in northern Persia, and by doing so to alienate the tribes faithful to the Shah who, with Western support, would then have drawn an impenetrable curtain over southern Persia; or to safeguard the unity of Iran and by doing so doom the communist elements to extinction. Moscow chose the latter alternative.

No sooner was the Azerbaijan crisis solved than the storm broke over Abadan. Supported by the bazaar, the lower clergy, and most of the intellectuals, Dr. Mossadegh seized power in May 1951, after the assassination of General Ali Razmara. The new regime promptly nationalized the oil wells, ex-propriating the British Anglo-Iranian Company. It took two years for the Shah, biding his time until a return of his popular favor had set in, to get rid of his turbulent, trouble-making minister.

Today, in the turmoil and ferment that have never ceased to reign in the Middle East since the war, the Shah is the only figure who represents continuity. By bringing their miserable living standards to his attention, the people at large trust that he will find ways and means of relieving them. Businessmen whose livelihood depends on stability and calm; officers eager to play again the part that fell to the Army under the dictatorship of the former Shah; and profoundly nationalist elements, who feel that only a strong monarchy can safeguard the unity and existence of the country—all look to the throne for salvation.

Three tamasha officers

21 For Tehranians in Gobineau's day, the military arts of Europe had made only one valid contribution to the betterment of the Persian armies: the *tamasha*. Whenever military parades were held, the crowd went into raptures over the ballet steps executed by the officers of the *tamasha*—what Frenchmen persist in calling *état-major* (and English and Americans, for some reason, "general staff"). Gobineau describes these staff officers: "Very nice-looking young fellows, dressed as handsomely as possible, mounted on fine horses, ride off in all directions at full speed; off they dart, back they come, and away again; it is a delight to see; to go dead slow is forbidden them, that would take all the pleasure out of the game; it is a very nice invention, God be praised."

Today the armed forces amount to eighty thousand men, not counting police and constabulary. Their commander in chief is the Shah.

The Iranian Army was the personal creation of Riza Shah Pahlevi, father of the present ruler. At the head of two thousand Cossacks, in 1921, Riza Shah drove the Kajars from the throne; on the Army his authority always rested. His son is in the same position: the Army is the one instrument on which he can rely unreservedly.

Only a national army directly dependent on the central power can keep the country together and firmly knit, for Iran is a mosaic of different tribes and races. The old Shah molded the Army into an instrument of national unification; he created its hierarchy and conferred on his best officers a nobility of the sword that took the place of nobility of birth.

All the young men of the country were called up for two years' military service, without any distinction of birth or class. Hundreds of officer candidates were sent to France and Germany for training in modern arms and tactics. By imbuing a whole generation of young Iranians with a sense of the national destinies, this reform went far beyond the military ranks.

When Dr. Mossadegh, after nationalizing the oil wells, took it into his head to try his strength against the Shah, the Army thwarted his efforts, first by paralyzing the action of the upstart government, then, with the support of a popular uprising, by overthrowing the Mossadegh regime on August 19, 1953.

Yet Mossadegh had succeeded in getting nominal control of the Army by filling the higher ranks with men of his own choosing and superimposing a governmental bureaucracy on the military organisms. But the Shah remained commander in chief of the armed forces, and the majority of officers remained steadfastly loyal to their young ruler, and deaf to the Siren overtures of the demagogue politician. Some units, moreover, such as the Imperial Guard, the frontier guards, and the constabulary, had not been affected by infiltration; they remained loyal to their commanding officers, and the latter to the king.

Throughout the Middle East the word *tamasha* is synonymous with agreeable disorder and frivolity. The word *état-major,* or general staff, has taken on new meaning, similar to the meaning it has in all modern armies.

Chapter Five

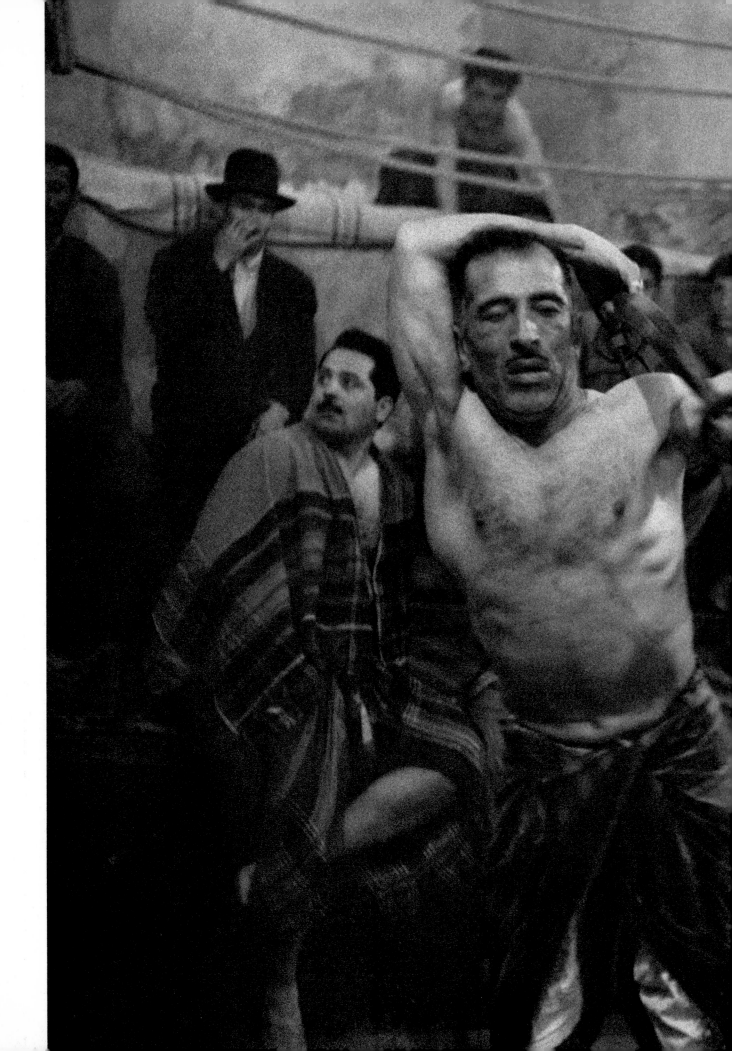

Knights of the muscle

22
23 Every morning at the stroke of six Shir Khoda, the famous gymnast, whose name means "the lion of God," transmits the formidable beat of his drum over the ether of Radio Tehran. For the athletes assembled in the *zurkhanehs,* the gymnasiums whose wall decorations glorify the exploits of national heroes, this is the signal for their daily exercises. These gymnastics, taking their rhythm from the strenuous manipulation of dumbbells, largely account for the vigor and fitness of the race in present-day Iran.

Actually the *zurkhaneh* serves mainly to develop the chest and arms. With their portly paunches and bulging muscles, these adepts look more like potbellied Japanese wrestlers than athletes molded in accordance with Greco-Roman canons of male beauty. As so often in the East, the sport practiced in the *zurkhaneh* is more like a piece of ritual choreography than actual physical exercises in our sense of the term. Its origins go back to the *pahlavans,* the legendary heroes of old akin to our knights of the Middle Ages. The Persians, as a matter of fact, have always maintained that medieval knighthood originated in their country.

The Turfan manuscripts, quoted by René Grousset in his *Empire of the Steppes,* allegedly prove that the Persian heroes wore the same dress as the Frankish knights. The *pahlavans* formed brotherhoods which wandered at large all over Central Asia, righting wrongs and warring against evil-doers. Their exploits gave rise to ballads and lays, and to characteristic dances which, originally the appanage of the nobles, are today current only among the lower classes.

The gymnasium is usually located in some dilapidated house in the bazaar. There, in a kind of pit in the center of a circular room, the *pahlavan,* which today means a gymnastics instructor, puts his pupils, his *nowchehs,* through their paces, while a *murshed* sets the rhythm to the beat of his drum.

Each performance proceeds in accordance with a carefully regulated ritual. The participants, barechested, with leather trunks, form a circle on the benches while awaiting their turn to step into the arena. The low door through which they enter the room compels them to bow down before saluting the onlookers.

The athlete begins by touching the floor with his finger tips, which he then lifts to his lips, then into the air, toward the sky visible through the glass dome of the ceiling. Next, to the beat of the drum, he juggles with the *mill,* huge wooden clubs. Others launch into an intricate dance with heavy chains, whose clanking accompanies the thumping of the drum.

"The athlete is an idle man," says a Persian proverb. That softening of the brain which has been known to be the lot of veteran boxers and wrestlers does not always spare the *pahlavan.* By dint of boasting of his strength and his muscles, he becomes in time, as age gains its hold on him, a bogus "bully of the neighborhood," but secretly admired an even "kept" by middle-aged ladies; he usually ends up as an opium or hashish addict. By then the strong man, who had gone so long by awe-inspiring nicknames (chosen by himself), such as Ahmed Gavgosh (ox killer), is no more than an object of popular ridicule, with a new nickname (chosen by others), such as Pahlavan Pembeh (cotton hero).

It often happens, however, that aging athletes in the poorer quarters find ready employment as thugs and cut-throats, available at a price for various dirty deeds, for a punitive expedition, for riots, raids, or what have you. Only a few years ago at Tehran, in the popular uprising that put an end to the Mossadegh regime, an important part was played by the henchmen of the *pahlavan* Shaban Bimokh (Shaban the slasher).

The Ethnographic Museum, Tehran

24 This costume museum was set up by a Persian novelist, Sanatizadeh Kermani. Rugs, miniatures, caftans, and headdresses of various persons are full of interest. But the wax figures are sometimes primitive. Iranians, one soon notices, are always afraid that foreigners will poke fun at this reconstitution of a recent past.

Chapter Six

Rug-making at Isfahan

25 Have you ever taken a good look at a Persian rug, from close range? The knots that go to make it up sometimes number several million. A good craftsman works at the rate of twelve hundred a day, and Iran is covered with rugs.

It is impossible to admire the gorgeous colors of a Tabriz or an Isfahan without recalling those impassible lads one sees in the workshops, tying, cutting, adjusting with unbelievable dexterity the many-colored threads of their loom, and never once lifting their huge dark eyes to the foreign visitors who watch them with amazement.

It is forbidden by law to employ children under fourteen. But in actual practice it is difficult to apply the law, birth certificates in so many cases being non-existent. Hence the surprisingly large proportion of workers not only under fourteen but even under ten; mere children, whose tiny fingers, however, lend themselves wonderfully to the meticulous work of rug-making, and whose pay need not be very high.

For each rug a particular pattern and color scheme are drawn up in advance. But very often the stitch and the thread to be used are designated in the course of a chant sung by the overseer.

Kilim at Isfahan

26 In every palace, as in the humblest home, a rug is on the floor. But the poor man's rug is the *kilim,* woven instead of knotted. Surrounded by her children, and using a rudimentary spinning wheel fed from skeins hanging on the wall behind her, this woman is making a *kilim,* which, though inferior to the knot-stitched rug on the loom in the background, will nevertheless form a harmonious and colorful carpet.

The rug is an indispensable accessory of Persian life: the poor man uses it to take his meals on, to sleep on, to pray on; on his rug he welcomes his guests. A different type and quality is peculiar to each region of Iran: the Tabriz is heavier and brightly colored; the Turkoman is made of coarse wool; the most costly of all is the Kerman, whose wool has the smooth suppleness of silk.

Images of the human figure are forbidden by the Moslem religion; for this reason down to the nineteenth century it appeared only in highly stylized forms. But since then popular art has resumed its traditions, and again kings, heroes, and pretty girls appear in certain patterns.

The carding room

27 Still today the beginning of cotton is carried out by means of a rudimentary beater: a thin catgut stretched between the two prongs of a small pitchfork. As always in Iran, the carder cannot put his heart into his work without chanting a rhyme tag or a snatch of a song. The vibration of the cord sets the pitch. The gist of his song is that he wants, not a woman to love and fondle, but a helpmate to share the hard day's work:

> *Pit! Pit! Pembeh!*
> *Baba manu zen deh!*
>
> *(Tap! Tap! Cotton!*
> *Father, get me a bride!)*

Silk-weaving at Yezd

28 The soil is so arid around the oasis of Yezd that food supplies have to be brought in from Isfahan and Kashan. Though its silk works have preserved a certain renown, they cannot be said to rival in fame or importance those at Challus and Resht on the Caspian.

The silk industry is a state monopoly—a lingering memory of the time when the Silk Route passed through Persia, when fine silks were a treasured commodity. Today, in Iran as elsewhere, nylon has done its devastating work. Deeply rooted traditions, however, ensure the livelihood of a good number of skilled silk workers.

Iran owes the creation of its modern industries to Riza Shah Pahlevi. When the Shah came to power in the twenties, the national economy depended almost entirely on agriculture, and even this was carried on by the most primitive means. The absence of specialized workers made the systematic mechanization of work all but impossible. Private capital much preferred real-estate speculation to any risky investments in industry.

This being so, the government was compelled to create state-owned companies in all sectors of the economy. Thereafter industrial development followed a steadily rising curve of growth, interrupted by the war; then came a certain stagnation, which lingered on until a few years ago. The soaring prosperity of the oil industry, bringing with it a new in-flux of foreign currency, had the effect of encouraging the importation of too many products with which local manufacturers could not possibly compete. Since 1955, energetic steps have been taken to improve the situation: import duties have been lifted on machinery and machine fittings; foreign investments can now be withdrawn at will from the country, and so can the profits on them. Long-term loans have been granted to encourage private industry, while the law now severely limits real-estate speculation and tends to channel unproductive capital toward industry.

Ghalamkars at Isfahan

29 Since time out of mind, Isfahan has been famous for its *ghalamkars,* its hand-painted textiles. With eighteen thousand spindles and several thousand mechanical looms, the Isfahan factories stand at the head of the Iranian cotton industry. The printed cotton fabrics seen here drying in the sun, in a courtyard at the bazaar, were produced on ancient looms; their bright patterns were printed from woodblocks.

Washing and scrubbing a rug

30 Again and again, threading his way through the crowded streets around the bazaar in some Iranian town, the exploring foreigner is suddenly brought up short and dares not take another step: there in front of him, covering the roadway and sidewalk, sumptuous woollen fabrics lie outspread, forming long, multicolored lanes. When the rug comes from the factory, its woollen fleece is still thick, too thick to appeal to discerning buyers. So the rug is unrolled in the middle of the street and exposed to dirt and weather, to the multitudinous feet of passers-by and animals, to the wheels of passing carts. After a few days it is taken in again, filthied but flattened. Then comes the final operation before it goes on sale: spread out beside a pool or stream, it is vigorously washed and scrubbed with *chubak,* a frothy mixture of sawdust, then tamped, flattened, and raked with a kind of hoe-shaped comb. As soon as it dries, it is shipped off to Europe or America, where careful housewives live in daily fear of the havoc wrought by a speck of dust or dirt.

Chapter Seven

31 Unquestionably one of the handsomest buildings in Isfahan is the Medresseyeh Madareh Shah, the Divinity School of the "Shah's Mother." Built two and a half centuries ago by the mother of Shah Safawid Sultan Hosain, the Medresseh is a masterwork of Persian architecture, with its great doorway inlaid with ceramic tiles, its cupola worked with enamelware stalactites, its gilded illuminations, its arcades, fountains, and vast prayer room.

Trained here are the men whose influence on the life of the nation has never waned in twelve centuries —the *mollahs,* in other words the "priests" of Shiite Mohammedanism.

The schooling of a *mollah* begins at the age of seven. The future priest enters on a period of study extending over twenty-one years, in the course of which his energies will be almost exclusively devoted to theology and Koranic law. He will learn the rudiments of arithmetic, nothing of science, next of to nothing of history.

The *talabehs* or divinity students never leave the Medresseh. They live at the expense of the community of believers, who feed and clothe them and load them with presents. On Thursday evenings, some of them season the monotony of study with a pleasant interlude. Women call and contract with them (out of charity, of course) what the Shiite law calls *sigheh* (temporary marriage). Their union, quite legitimate, lasts an evening or an hour or two, just as they wish. And having benefited by this *savab kardan* (good deed), the seminarist resumes his studies the next morning.

They take their finishing course in one of the two Shiite universities, either at Kum, near Tehran, or at Nejef in Iraq. After that the new *mollah* receives a diploma from the hands of the *mujtahed,* the principal Shiite Imam. He then has the right to beg alms and distribute *fatwas,* documents in which he expresses his opinion on matters submitted to him.

Each *mollah* keeps a school, like the master clerics of the Middle Ages, and teaches a certain number of students, who at the same time act as his servants. The authorities have recently begun granting scholarships to them. They also live on the life interest of property bequeathed to them by charitable souls.

There are scarcely more than a thousand genuine *mollahs* in the whole of Iran. But if we include divinity students (of whom there were lately reckoned to be five thousand in Kum alone) and charlatans, their number easily exceeds twenty thousand. No one can prevent a Moslem from wearing a black turban, the distinctive sign of the *mollah*, or a white one, denoting a sheik, or a green one, denoting a member of a religious brotherhood. It is left to the public to distinguish the true from the false.

But the public is not always capable of discriminating. No wonder, then, that it is often the dupe of impostors who stir up the mob in pursuance of their own schemes. A *mollah*, for example, will wage a campaign, and most effectively, against a commercial product to which he has taken a dislike. Others stirred up the populace in 1951 against the British oil company, in 1953 against Mossadegh.

To understand the part played by *mollahs* in Iran, one has to know something about the essential dogma of Shiite Islam with respect to the temporal authority. Unlike the majority of Moslems (who are Sunnites), the Shiites carry the origin of religious power back to Ali (son-in-law of the Prophet) and his successors, the Imams. Since the last of the legitimate Imams, the Mahdi, has lived in hiding for several centuries now, no legitimate power can exist on the earth until such time as he reappears.

The *mollahs* accordingly lay claim to all rights and powers in the name of the hidden Imam: the exclusive, unimpeachable right to interpret the Koran and Koranic tradition, the power to administer justice in compliance with Koranic law, and so on.

From there to judging the acts of the temporal power and imposing their own views on every event of political life, there was only a step, and the *mollahs* took it unhesitatingly. And so the men in black turbans flatter now the rich, who pay for their upkeep, now the poor, who are the instruments of their power.

The *mollahs* originally formed a cultivated and enlightened elite. Nowadays, with a few exceptions, they are grossly ignorant and unprincipled. Some of the most daring satires and vignettes in the popular tradition stigmatize the amorality of cynical and hypocritical *mollahs*.

Since the revolution carried out by the previous Shah, the awe-inspiring Riza Pahlevi, the *mollahs* have lost much of their influence. Determined to lift his country out of the Middle Ages, the Shah went to great lengths to modernize the Persian way of life. He broke the power of the black-turbaned priests who formed the really backward element in Iran. He issued *firmans* (imperial decrees) suppressing the veil covering women's faces, forbidding the wearing of turbans and the traditional headdresses, and even restricting the wearing of beards.

But the religious tradition has remained very much alive. The *mollahs* still keep their seats at the imperial Salam, when all the state dignitaries rise and bow to the Shah. Their sermons still resound in the mosques and on the radio, and nearly all the ceremonies of social life require their presence.

And during the two Moslem months of Muharram and Saphar, especially, the *mollah* regains all his prestige. At that period, each year, Iran goes into mourning. The faithful flock to the mosques where preachers tell in detail the story of the tragedy of Kerbela, which for Shiite Moslems is the holiest place in the world.

Thirteen centuries ago Hosain and Hassan, grandsons of the Prophet Mohammed, had their throats cut at Kerbela, in the Mesopotamian desert, by the followers of Yazid. Their martyrdom, which forms the very basis of the beliefs of Shiite Moslems, is commemorated on Ashura, the tenth day of Muharram, a day of public mourning, and the people, keyed up to fever pitch, drink in the interminable recital of luridly colored details: "Hosain shall come to Mecca!... There he is at Kerbela!... Tomorrow shall he be killed.... He falls dead!... Yesterday he died!"

The long account of these events fills the hearts of believers all over Iran with tearful compassion, and gives the *mollah* an opportunity of parading his learning and playing on the emotions of his listeners.

Isfahan: the Friday mosque

32 The Masjedeh Jomeh, the "Friday mosque," is probably one of the oldest monuments of Isfahan, and unquestionably one of the loveliest. Its oldest parts go back to the eleventh, possibly even to the ninth century. The nucleus of the building is a masterpiece of the Seljuk period, but each succeeding dynasty made a point of adding something of its own, enlarging and embellishing it. As a result it now amounts to a kind of cross section of Persian Islamic art, with its zigzag arcades, its sculptured plaster work, its marvelous mosaics of enameled tiles, its cupolas fretted with stalactites, its colonnades and minarets.

At each cardinal point of the vast central court stands an *iwam*, a monumental porch giving access to a prayer room. The Koran enjoins five prayers a day on the pious Moslem. He is free to say his prayers wherever he chooses (except on graves or in impure places): at home, in the fields, even in the street. But custom requires that on Fridays he should repair to a mosque for his prayers. "O you who believe! When you are summoned to prayers on Friday, hasten to comply with the invocation of Allah and leave your affairs!" (Koran, LXII, 9).

In all the cities of Iran the Friday mosque is generally the largest and most handsomely decorated. There the local notabilities are to be seen, and the *Imam jomeh,* the Friday preacher, is considered to be the most pious Moslem of the community.

Facing the *mirhab,* a profusely decorated niche indicating the *kibla,* the direction of Mecca, and led by the Imam, who stands at the head of the congregation, the faithful perform the consecrated rites, then listen to the sermon, which the preacher delivers squatting on the *minbar,* a platform beside the *mirhab.*

A *masjed,* or mosque, is not only a place of pious worship and prayer. With its inner gardens, its ablution fountains, its seminary where the *mollahs* distribute alms to the poor, its shady courtyards and cool vestibules, the mosque attracts a steady stream of beggars and loafers all day long, who doze in the sun, eat a frugal meal, and gossip and argue with one another. Here the dead are laid out pending burial. The hours glide by and the day wanes, broken at intervals by the singsong of prayers and sermons.

The sermons touch on every conceivable subject, from daily life to the hole war against the infidel. The preacher delivers it without a pause or break, droning on in a monotonous tone. As often as not he has nothing particular to say. A typical example is the *mollah* we heard one day at Isfahan, whose sermon ran something like this: "I know a Moslem who has no shoes, a Moslem who has no shirt, a Moslem who has no headdress. What would you have him do? This Moslem must be provided with shoes, shirt, headdress. . . ." On and on it went in this strain.

The assembled crowd reacts as a rule in various ways. Some doze, some listen without registering what they hear, stupefied by the heat, too busy driving away the flies and insects. Others fall into the rhythm of the sermon and keep time with a nodding of the head.

Now and then one man will show a keen interest in what is being said. Afterward, on the way out, he improvises a commentary in a loud voice, taking up the thread of the preacher's argument and harangu-ing the crowd. Thus public opinion is born. The *mollah,* very likely, will join this fresh discussion and launch into a political tirade. Even today neither the police nor the Army has the right to enter a sanctuary. Here, as in the churches of Europe in the Middle Ages, both the criminal and the political refugee find inviolable asylum. The "outlaw" enjoys the privilege of remaining within the precincts of the mosque as long as he likes, fed by the faithful and visited by family and friends, until the *mollahs* and the community can intercede in his favor and obtain an *aman,* a pardon.

During Ramadan (the ninth month of the Moslem year, devoted to strict fasting) the mosques are full for other reasons: most believers then prefer the contemplative to the active life, as it whets the appetite to a lesser degree. The mosques are so crowded at this time of year that each family makes a point of sending in the children as early as possible with the shoes of the whole family, so as to reserve room for them all; with the result that innumerable disputes arise, and rival families may be seen loudly claiming priority and vehemently pointing to rows of shoes.

Pray to Allah standing, sitting, or reclining

33 Saying prayers is one of the five obligations of the practicing Moslem. With alms-giving, it is his most important duty, the one on which the Koran lays most stress.

Five times a day, after duly purifying himself by bathing or washing, the believer performs *sahla.* He turns first toward Mecca, then marks out a small space on the ground in which to isolate himself from the outer world. This space is usually defined automatically by the rug on which he stands.

Then, standing up and holding his hands level with his shoulders, he pronounces the words *Allah Akbar* (God is great); lowering his hands he recites the *fatha;* he bends over with his palms against his knees for the *roku,* stands erect again for the *yehtidal,* and then lies prone with his nose against the ground for the *sojud,* intently absorbed all the while in the entreaty addressed to his God.

During his prayers a fervent Moslem loses all sense of his earthly surroundings, rising in spirit toward the heavenly paradise promised by the Koran, transformed into a *shahid,* which signifies at once a witness, a saint, and a martyr to the faith.

His world is his carpet, be it ever so humble, on

which he presses his forehead and murmurs his ardent wishes for happiness, wealth, power. The fabulous flying carpet of the *Thousand and One Nights* has no other origin but this.

Certain Shiite Moslems add to the rug a *mohr,* or "prayer brick," on which they press their face while saying the *sojud.* The *mohr* is supposed to be made of the clay dug from the *turbats,* the places where saints are buried. But rumor has it that more than one of these objects of piety are made of clay which comes straight from the garden of an enterprising *mollah* who does a thriving business in prayer bricks.

The world's most beautiful square

34 So it is called at Isfahan, and not without reason. This square is the delight of tourists, whether they come from the West or from the Arab world, like these three visitors in black, being shown around the city by an adolescent guide.

Maidaneh Shah is its name—the Shah's Square of the days when Isfahan was still the capital of the Empire. Sir John Chardin, describing it three centuries ago, saw it "covered with tradesmen selling their wares on mats and leaving them unguarded at night, merely wrapped up or placed in chests." On the square the lords of the realm played their favorite game, polo. There the Shah gave entertainments and held executions. When evening came, the tradesmen gave way to "charlatans, puppet shows, conjurors, storytellers, preachers, and the tents of dissolute women." At night, all around the buildings on the square, "resounding to the appalling din of long trumpets and huge kettledrums, three times greater in diameter than ours, public rejoicings take place amid high poles hung with fifty thousand earthenware lamps and providing the finest illumination in the world."

Such were the splendors Isfahan enjoyed some forty years before Versailles was built, but they have long since vanished. The Maidan, nevertheless, is still the most popular public promenade in the city. The square forms an immense parallelogram, 560 yards long and 174 yards wide, bordered with recessed arcades, one above the other, connecting the monuments which dominate the square: the Masjedeh Shah, the "Shah's mosque," with a fabulous blue dome from which the Shahs used to observe the crowds surging in the square below; the graceful mosque of Sheik Lutfallah; the Kaysari, the Imperial Bazaar, with its monumental entrance gate.

Chardin gave a lengthy enumeration of the wonders of the Imperial palace, a league and a half in circumference, with its gates of green porphyry, its so-called "drawing rooms in the stables" reserved for foreign ambassadors amid a garden of huge plane trees, embellished with marble pools and fountains; its throne room with three ornamental lakes superimposed, its eighteen gilded columns thirty feet high, its walls of white marble painted and gilded halfway up, with the rest of colored crystal. The harem, an enchanted place made for the delight of the senses, was more than a league in circumference. The walls were so high that no monastery in Europe can show the like.

All around the Shah's Square Isfahan unfolds its gardens, and its wonderful monuments whose minarets and cupolas stand out against a background of mountains.

Isfahan is inseparably associated with the name of Shah Abbas, the contemporary of Henry IV and Louis XIII in France and Queen Elizabeth and James I in England. He welded Persia into a unified whole, and his long reign, lasting from 1587 to 1629, was Persia's Golden Age. French travelers who visited the Empire under this great monarch record that, whenever they marveled at a monument or questioned the Persians as to its origin, the reply was invariably the same: Shah Abbas had it erected. Hence, no doubt, the recurring pleasantry in Perrault's tale of "Puss in Boots," in which everything always belongs to Carabas.

Shah Abbas was the third sovereign of the Safawid Dynasty, which in the early sixteenth century succeeded in freeing Persia from the triple yoke of the Arabs, Turks, and Mongols. The first two Shahs of the new line, Ismail and Tahmasp, had conquered western Persia; Shah Abbas took over and completed the task of liberation.

When he mounted the throne Shah Abbas was only sixteen. Yet from the very outset he showed a profound knowledge of the art of government and of military tactics. The first Safawid ruler, Shah Ismail, had skillfully used the Shiite sect as a political instrument against the Sunnite Turks. The Shiites, let it be remembered, are Moslems who refuse to acknowledge the legitimacy of the first three Caliphs, Abu Bakr, Omar, and Osman, the immediate successors of Mohammed, as commanders of the faithful. For the Shiites, the only true Caliphs are those who descended from Ali, son-in-law of Mohammed and fourth Caliph. Until the time of Shah Ismail, the Shiite sect had rallied only a scattered body of adherents, disunited and devoid of political influence. Ismail imposed Shiism on Persia, and by this means sharply differentiated Persians from other Moslems, thus enabling them to preserve their national character intact in the face of foreign invasions.

Shah Abbas consolidated the work of his predecessors. After driving the Uzbeks out of Khurasan in 1597, he compelled the Turks to evacuate Azerbaijan in 1603. Alive to the danger represented by the latent hostility of the Ottomans, he concluded a truce with them, and refrained for the time being from driving them out of the peripheral provinces. To pacify and placate them (for they were Sunnites), he consented to suppress throughout his Empire the curse against the first three Caliphs in the Shiite prayer ritual.

Free now to devote himself to unifying his country, he began by transferring the capital from Kazvin to Isfahan. He built up a powerful military machine. Thanks to two English adventurers, Sir Anthony Shirley and Sir Robert Shirley, his artillery had no rival in the East. He strengthened his infantry with regiments of converted Armenians and Georgians, and, following the example of the Ottomans, he created a guard unit of Turkish Janizaries. When he felt himself strong enough, he took the offensive.

Breaking the truce of 1618, he finished driving the Turks out of Mesopotamia in 1623 and occupied Georgia. With the help of an English squadron of the East India Company, he captured the islands of the Persian Gulf from the Portuguese and founded the port of Bandar Abbas. He was the first Persian leader to realize that the only way to strengthen the Empire was to enlist Europe and Christendom on his side. He accordingly sent the Shirley brothers to solicit the support of the European powers. A Roman gentleman passing through Persia was prevailed on to lead an expedition against the Portuguese. Farsighted and modern-minded, Shah Abbas never hesitated to call in foreigners whenever he thought his subjects stood to benefit by their presence or example. When the Armenians were being persecuted in the rest of the Moslem world, he welcomed them in his Empire. For them, at Isfahan, he built the suburb of Julfa (which takes its name from the town on the Araxes, in Azerbaijan, whence the Armenians came) and granted them full rights and privileges, even the privilege of building their own churches and worshiping in their own way. The coming of these Armenians to Julfa proved to be of capital importance for Persia: first-rate craftsmen, architects, and engineers, they contributed in large measure to build the sights of Isfahan. They formed commercial ties with Christendom, to the great advantage and enrichment of their community and their adopted country.

Shah Abbas carried religious tolerance to the point of allowing foreign monasteries to be established in Persia. He welcomed a group of Carmelites and encouraged other orders, which for the first time enabled Persian youth to learn of the outside world.

Shah Abbas did not confine himself to embellishing his capital with palaces, gardens, and bridges. He had rivers deflected in order to improve the water supply. He built roads and did his utmost to guarantee the security of communications by waging a ruthless war against brigands and highway robbers. He gave a new impetus to the intellectual life of Persia by patronizing scholars, poets, and philosophers.

When he had once decided on a project, he carried it through undeterred by scruples. Chardin tells how the largest caravanserai in Isfahan was built by an oil merchant at the "suggestion" of Shah Abbas. The Shah condescended to pay a personal visit to the wealthy tradesman and discreetly placed him before the following alternative: either to draw up his will in his sovereign's favor or to build the caravanserai. The oil merchant, as might be expected, opted for the latter solution.

The Shah's cruelty is as legendary as his greatness. Uneasy at the growing power of Kuli Khan, his first vizier, to whom in fact he owed his own elevation, he had no hesitation about having him assassinated. In the same way he executed his eldest son, Sufi Mirza, who had become too popular for his liking. Insubordination had only to show its head to be mercilessly punished. This brutality, however, is to some extent accounted for by the anarchic state of affairs when he ascended the throne. Stern measures were called for after the centuries of invasions and massacres through which Persia had just passed.

So in spite of the severity of his government, Shah Abbas still lives today in the hearts of his countrymen as the greatest monarch of the Persian Renaissance. His century in Persia, like that of Louis XIV in France, takes its name from him—the century of Abbas the Great.

What prince can boast of a finer epitaph than the one Sir John Chardin coined for Shah Abbas: "When he ceased to live, Persia ceased to prosper"?

Chapter Eight

35 What now remains of the power of the Magi who once dominated Persia and the East? Much of their lore, in any case, has been inherited by such old women as this one, pacing slowly between the mud-walled cottages of the tiny village of Sham, near Yezd.

When the victorious Arabs imposed Mohammedanism on the peoples of Persia in the seventh century, the Zoroastrians who refused to be converted were reduced to the condition of miserable outcasts; their belongings were ruthlessly confiscated, in accordance with Koranic law, and distributed to those who adopted Mohammedanism. The Ghebers (as Zoroastrian fire worshipers are called) as a whole were a land-owning class, but almost all who remained faithful to their traditional religion were dispossessed and ruined. "From then on," writes Gobineau, "they were oppressed not so much because they were infidels but because they were paupers."

Today the Ghebers live apart in villages of their own. Those who remain in the large cities have been able to maintain a certain standing, and a modest prosperity, only by submitting outwardly to the laws of Islam. All Ghebers are looked down upon by Moslems for holding what the latter dismiss as childish superstitions. But Persians today are so proud of their past, so proud of a national history that spans several thousand years, that they have come to regard the descendants of the Zoroastrian Magi as living symbols of the ancient grandeur of their country.

Gheber village near Yezd

36 Like the Jews in the ghettos of prewar Europe, the fire-worshiping Ghebers have had to live apart from the main community for centuries in order to practice their religion in their own way. As a rule, up to now, they have lived in compact, out-of-the-way villages. City-dwelling Ghebers nearly always live in houses surrounded by high thick walls.

The region around Yezd is well known for its torrid summers. But the domes surmounting Gheber houses effectively keep the interior cool and ventilated. These people earn their living as craftsmen. The heads of the community are the priests or *Mobeds,* better known in the West as "Magi." Gheber tradition has it that the "three wise men from the East" who, guided by a star, paid homage to Christ at His nativity were not kings of different countries but three Magi, priests of the fire-worshiping religion.

Altar of fire at Sham

37 The sacred obligation to keep a flame forever burning has given the Ghebers a profound knowledge of the properties of fire. All the handicrafts requiring a skilled use of fire are usually practiced by Ghebers; they are unsurpassed as goldsmiths, jewelers, plumbers, and so on. The flame that purifies the soul of the Zoroastrian adept also helps him earn his livelihood.

Offerings to Ormuzd

38 Ormuzd being the god and creator of good, Persians customarily pay him honor by offering him the good things of the earth: fruit, flowers, vegetables, clear water, perfumes, and cakes. All this, needless to say, is grouped around oil lamps in which the purifying flame steadily burns.

Zoroastrian superstitions remain very much alive in Persia even today, not only among the Ghebers but even in old Persian families converted centuries ago to the Mohammedan faith. Gobineau writes: "When a man dies, it is not unusual in certain families to shut and lock the doors, taking good care to be safe from prying eyes. Then a burner is lit beside the death bed and incense burned. When the smoke curls up, a precious book, kept carefully hidden except on these occasions, is taken out and passed several times through the cloud of smoke. Sometimes this book consists of no more than a few loose pages: it is the Zend-Avesta or a remnant of it. None of the persons present is capable of reading it or even knows what is in it. Yet all regard this mysterious relic as the most sacred object in the world. As soon as this ceremony is over, the remaining funeral rites are performed in the Moslem manner."

Thus Spake Zarathustra . . .

39 The *Adesh-kadeh*, the altar of fire. In every Gheber home there is a consecrated hearth in which a flame perpetually burns. The Zoroastrian religion originated in Azerbaijan (which means "land of fire").

Now it is a fact that even today in this region, as in Iraqian Kurdistan, open fires are often to be found burning on the ground; this is the natural combustion of gas from oil deposits, and has been taking place in this manner for untold centuries. Childless women walk on hot coals in the belief that fire will consume their sterility. For a Zoroastrian adept a promise made before a flame is sacred.

The doctrine taught by Zoroaster in the sacred book of the Zend-Avesta consists in the permanent struggle between two elements: Ormuzd (the principle of light and good) and Ahriman (the principle of darkness and evil). Their opposing hosts of spirits endlessly contend for possession of souls. The final battle between them is expected to be fought in the year 2345, when the Messiah will appear and the earth will be purified by a flood of molten metal. Then the Last Judgment will take place.

Meanwhile, men's eternal souls are weighed at death by three judges. The weighing takes place, however, only after a period of astral wandering, until finally the soul comes to a bridge. If the scales tip to the good side, the bridge widens out before it and leads the soul to a region of felicity and eternal light. If the scales remain in equal balance, the soul is consigned to a place of purification (purgatory). If they tip to the evil side, then the soul is led down an ever narrower bridge and finally sinks out of sight forever in irremediable chaos.

Weaving at Sham

40 Old looms, with their old secrets of fine weaving. This Zoroastrian woman is working with coarse material (she can afford nothing better), but the end result will be a piece of work which no foreigner can see without the deepest admiration.

The children's dinner

41 *Ash khobeh!* "The soup tastes good!" These are Zoroastrian children. If they were Moslems, their heads would be shaved clean. Persian cooking, even in the humblest homes, has a variety and relish that delight foreigners—whose enthusiasm, however, is usually a little damped when popular courtesy requires them to eat out of a common plate with the rest of the family.

Chapter Nine

44

42 The southern part of the country, Fars or Pars, witnessed the rise of the first empire of the ancient Persians, from whom the whole country was destined to take its name. There, from Persepolis to Pasargadae, from Shiraz to Firuzabad, ancient Persia and modern Iran meet and mingle, but without ever quite merging into each other. The old traditions have been handed down from the Achaemenians to the Pahlevis, in spite of invasions, foreign domination, and the ravages of time. Alongside city dwellers, the nomads continue to lead their life of wanderlust. Though always on the march in never-ending caravan treks, the girls of the nomad tribes can easily hold their own in elegance and smartness with their sisters in the cities. This Parsee beauty belongs to a tribe of the Baziris region.

"All the kingdoms of the earth hath the Lord God of heaven given me."—II Chronicles, 36:23.

43 Thus spoke Cyrus, king of Persia, and his words, recorded in the Old Testament, strangely re-echo the song of glory which the great Achaemenian king had engraved on a cylinder seal: "When I made a peaceful entrance into Babylon, Marduk, the great god to whom I prayed daily, opened the hearts of the Babylonians to me. My numerous soldiery filed quietly through the city. I freed the inhabitants of a yoke which had weighed heavily on them. I am Cyrus, King of the Universe, the great and powerful King of Babylon, Sumer, and Akkad, King of the Four Quarters of the World."

Pasargadae was built by Cyrus the Great in 550 B.C. The only vestige of the place which has escaped destruction is this tomb, supposed to be the king's own. It consists of a sarcophagus chamber raised on a limestone pyramid. But the tomb pillagers have done their worst, from the traitorous satrap strangled by Alexander to the Fars nomads of the present day, who have plundered all the archeological treasures of the region.

Nothing, moreover, could be more uncertain than the authenticity of this royal tomb; Cyrus, after all, was a Zoroastrian—an adept, that is, of a cult which allows the dead to be neither buried nor entombed, but exposes them to carrion-eating birds so as not to befoul the elements by direct contact with dead flesh. The Moslem conquerors who overran Persia called this monument the "tomb of Solomon's mother," and by adding to it an Islamic *mirhab* incorporated it outright into the Moslem heritage.

Tombs of the Sassanian Kings

44 Herdsmen and their flocks from all over the region forgather here at a watering place at the foot of the mountains dominating Persepolis: above, hewn out of the rock face, are the tombs of Sassanian kings.

At the death of Alexander the Great in 323 B.C., his generals divided the empire between them: Antigonus kept Greece, Ptolemy received Egypt, and Seleucus took Asia. The Seleucid Dynasty reigned for about a century, spreading the Greek way of life, improving the backward provinces, and building cities. Gradually its kings withdrew from Persia and —as if under the spell of homesickness—moved closer to the shores of the Mediterranean. Antiochus founded his capital in Syria. At last, defeated by the Romans, harried by an outburst of Asiatic nationalism and increasing hostility against everything Greek, the Seleucids lost Persia in 247 B.C. and were replaced by the Parthian dynasty of the Arsacids. The reign of the latter, however, lasted only thirty years. The empire was in the throes of anarchy when the last Arsacid king, Artabanus V, was defeated and killed by the founder of the Sassanian Dynasty, Ardashir.

The rule of the Sassanians was to last eight and half centuries, the longest continuous period in the history of ancient Persia. The Persians have now been Moslems for thirteen centuries. But no period of his country's past is more admired by the average Persian than that of the pre-Islamic dynasty of the Sassanians. The hardy kings of that age, who emerged from the desert wastes of the south, are half-legendary figures; their exploits, familiar in song and myth to all Iranians, are carved in the rock at Naksh-i-Rustam, near Shiraz. The Sassanians boldly waged war against the greatest power on earth at that time, the Roman Empire, and routed its armies more than once. Shapur I defeated the Emperor Valerianus at Edessa and reduced the Roman legions to slavery. Khosrau II captured Jerusalem and carried off the True Cross, which Queen Boran restored to the Byzantine Emperor.

Between Bushire and Shiraz, Shapur I founded a city bearing his name. The Sassanians reorganized the Empire. Impressive ruins at Ctesiphon on the Tigris, at Kasr-Shirin, and on the frontier between Iran and Iraq testify to the greatness of the dynasty.

Roman prisoners were employed to build roads, and bridges and dams on the Karun. The Dizful bridge is 1250 feet long, the one at Shuster 1130 feet long. To build the Shuster dam Shapur had to deflect a river; each day, in the course of the construction work, two thousand ewes supplied the milk which went to mix the mortar.

But the reign of the Sassanians was a time of intense religious ferment. Shapur made Mazdaism the state religion and had commentaries on the Zend-Avesta written in the vulgar tongue which, however, show the strong influence of Greek and Hindu ideas. But the new doctrine born in Persia was rapidly diffused throughout the Empire. At first Shapur tolerated Christianity; his successors, however, under the influence of the Zoroastrian Magi, embarked on a campaign of persecution and massacred the Armenian Christians. New sects gradually sprouted from the main stem of Mazdaism. Mani, born in 215 A.D. in Mesopotamia, preached Manichaeism, a monotheistic form of Mazdaism with which he mingled the Christian notions of baptism and communion, condemning sacrifices and recognizing Christ as the Messiah. Saint Augustine was a Manichaean in his youth, before being converted to Catholicism. The Zoroastrian Magi had Mani crucified and skinned alive in 275, but his doctrines spread to India and Egypt. The Crusaders brought them back from the East in the twelfth century, and they gave rise to the Albigensian heresy in France.

In the fifth century another illuminee, Mazdak, went about preaching and prophesying the advent of a communistic society in which property and land (and women) would be shared in common and belong to no one in particular. His pronouncements led to unrest and riots; King Kavah had Mazdak put to death and peace was restored.

The Sassanians proceeded to organize a Zoroastrian priesthood of Magi and *Mobeds,* who in time became all-powerful. Society was broken up into four distinct classes or castes: priests, warriors, scribes, and, at the bottom of the scale, poor and oppressed, the peasants and craftsmen.

Pending their deliverance from serfdom, the Persian people built cities and palaces for their stern taskmasters. The ruins of Persepolis provided the material for the construction of Istakhar, a few miles from the old Achaemenian city. In the Temple of Fire, dedicated to the goddess Anahit, the Sassanian kings hung up the heads of their enemies and of any

Christians who fell into their hands. There an eternal flame burned on the altars of Zoroaster. One night, according to legend, the flame went out—an evil omen for the Magi. Somewhere, in the heart of Arabia, Mohammed had just been born.

The Arabs began filtering into Persia in the first half of the seventh century. In 642 the marauding bands of Caliph Omar turned on Persia, forced a way over the Zagros mountains, and crushed the troops of Yazdegerd, the last Sassanian king. From then on Persia was a Moslem country. A new era had dawned: by embracing Islam, and by the contact thus established with the Moslem world, Persia was able to exert an influence on art, literature, and thought which soon extended throughout the East and even penetrated into Europe by way of Spain.

The people of the steppes

45
46 Red and black tents, the camps of the nomads, dot the steppes which form three quarters of Iran's total land area. These camps are peopled by all the races which in the course of centuries have swept down toward the fertile plains of Khurasan and the palatial cities of the Irak-Ajami and Fars provinces. Even today, in touring the country, you will meet Turkoman riders in the Gurgan and along the Caspian, Turkish nomads in Azerbaijan, Kurds all along the western frontier, Baluch and Afghan tribes in the east, Lurs and Bakhtiari in the oil-well zones, and Arab Bedouins in the south (to whom the region owes its present name: Arabistan).

The most dramatic episodes in the history of these regions have been enacted by these peoples who, as René Grousset says, have remained at the pastoral stage of civilization, while all the rest of Asia has long since reached the most advanced agricultural stage.

Today the wild forays of Khirgiz horsemen, of Scyths and Turkomans, continue to form the theme and subject matter of the chants and tales so avidly listened to in the long nightly vigils around nomad fires. And under the torrid sun of southern Persia the shepherds and herdsmen who descend from the Turk and Mongol conquerors of old still trek from watering place to watering place, like their forebears.

Anxious to bolster the authority of the central government, Riza Shah Pahlevi broke the political power of the clan chieftains who for centuries had dominated the peripheral areas of the Empire. But social problems remain to be solved. On the whole,

the nomads subsist on the produce of their flocks. Some tribes, such as the Kassemabadis of the Caspian, live by hunting and fishing. Others, such as the Zolfaghazis in the north and the Kashgais in the south, cooperate occasionally with the Tehran authorities, whenever they can make it worth their while. Still others, in Kurdistan, do a thriving business as smugglers. More and more members of these tribes, though seldom abandoning their nomadic way of life, seek part-time employment in industry—for example, the Bakhtiari families at Abadan.

The origin of certain tribes, such as the Kolis pictured here camping on the outskirts of Tehran, remains a mystery. Gypsies in all probability, they wander up and down the country, exhibiting wild animals, putting on folk plays, doing odd jobs or menial service for as long as they can bear to stay in one place; then they take their meager wages and move on. They are tinkers, and villagers on their route bring them any pots or pans that need mending. Nearly all the actual work is left to women; the men lead an idle life, and it is not an uncommon sight to see one of them on the bank of a stream being washed and scrubbed by his wife. The Kolis on the whole have the reputation of honesty, but city dwellers keep their valuables under lock and key whenever a tribe of them comes to town, acting on the Persian proverb which says "An open door invites a thief."

Paradise lost

47
48 Biblical tradition locates the Garden of Eden somewhere between Fars and Khuzistan. There is nothing now to help the imagination form any idea of that earthly paradise. However, the nomad caravans, moving with the seasons across this bleak country, still resemble those described in the Bible.

The world bowed down in worship here

49 Pasargadae is in sight. These foothills, twenty-five centuries ago, were the seat of empire. Nubian slaves, jewelers from India, Zoroastrian Magi and Hebrew doctors, Greek craftsmen and Scythian mercenaries, all the races of the known world contributed to the grandeur of the Achaemenian kings. It is not unusual today for a Fars camel driver, as he pitches his tent for the night, to drive his peg into a solid object and bring to light a statuette or a bronze that the hand of Cyrus might once have touched.

Chapter Ten

50 A few blocks of stone and a shattered statue, remnants of a metropolis that was once the hub of the world. Twenty-six centuries lie between present-day Iran and the epic age of the Achaemenian Persians. For the young Iranian of today, however, there is no discontinuity between an age that saw the Empire of the World in the hands of his ancestors and modern times.

The first great Persian Empire, dating from the sixth century B.C., was that of the Achaemenians, stretching from Nubia to the Indus, from Ethiopia to Central Asia. In 558 B.C. Cyrus II mounted the throne of the small kingdom of Susa and rebelled against his overlord, the king of the Medes, who reigned at Ecbatana (present-day Hamadan). This was the beginning of an ascension which led the Achaemenian Dynasty to dominate the ancient world until the year 331 B.C., when Alexander the Great appeared on the scene. The Achaemenians built up an empire covering Persia, India, Transoxiana, Asia Minor, Mesopotamia, Syria, Egypt, Thrace, Macedonia, and Ionia. The names of these empire builders have come down to us in the writings of the Greek historians: Cyrus, conqueror of Babylon and protector of the Jewish people; Cambyses, the inspired madman who conquered Egypt and had himself worshiped like a Pharaoh; Darius the Great; Xerxes, inglorious winner at Thermopylae, soundly beaten on the Hellespont and at Salamis and Plataea; lastly, Darius III, who succumbed to Alexander the Great.

The Persian Empire was, for ancient times, a model of fair and tolerant administration. It was divided into twenty-three provinces. In each the King of Kings was represented by three officials: the governor, the satrap, and a security officer commanding the armed forces. Each of these officials was directly responsible to the king for the welfare of the province. To keep a watch on things, special inspectors called "the eyes and ears of the king" were constantly on the move from province to province, invested with sweeping powers and protected by a strong bodyguard. A word from them was enough to destitute a satrap guilty of mismanagement, and even to have him executed without being brought to trial.

The satrap kept law and order and collected taxes. With the help of the armed forces, he was responsible for the security of the roads, for the protection of crops, and for the inviolability of the royal hunting reserves. The latter were known as *paridaiza,* from which our word "paradise" derives. The royal justice was renowned for its severity and dispatch. Any judge convicted of accepting bribes was flayed alive and strips of his flesh were draped over the bench of justice, on which the victim's sons, as an object lesson, were then compelled to sit. Corporal punishment of various kinds—of which castration and blinding were the mildest—were inflicted mercilessly for the least offense against the king's law.

In spite of this streak of cruelty, typical of the age, the Achaemenian rulers were certainly the most enlightened of their time. From Darius the Great to Darius III, the ancient world enjoyed the *pax persica,* two centuries of peace and prosperity during which the arts flourished as never before. The courts of Susa and Persepolis attracted craftsmen from every country. Achaemenian art was not an original creation: it borrowed its columns, capitals, and bas-reliefs from the Greeks, Egyptians, and Assyrians. Most of its masterpieces were the handiwork of foreign masons, architects, goldsmiths, and jewelers. But the dynasty did things on a large scale: all the constructions bearing its distinctive mark are colossal. The sights they had seen in Upper Egypt seemed to haunt the Persian conquerors. As no temples were required by the Zoroastrian cult, they covered their empire with palaces and cities of stone linked to one another by royal highways, vestiges of which are still visible today.

Persepolis: the Apadana of Darius and Xerxes

51
52 Set on fire by Alexander the Great at the desire (the
53 story goes) of Thais, the lovely courtesan, Persepolis, the capital of the Achaemenian Empire, is no more

today than a scattered heap of ruins—but ruins impressive and evocative in the highest degree. Instead of building with the sun-dried bricks of the Assyrians (which have all crumbled to dust), the Persians used stone. Victorious over centuries of destruction and pillage, over raiding Mongol horsemen and earthquakes, the gigantic terrace of Persepolis still lifts its mighty columns to the sky. The eight surviving columns are nearly ninety feet high. The irregular blocks of stone neatly fitted together to form the base of the terrace are strikingly well preserved. Each building, or what remains of it, is decorated with relief sculptures of animals four times life-size.

The monumental double flight of stairs leading to the terrace is made of enormous blocks of carefully hewn freestone. It rises at a low angle so as to allow horsemen to ride up without dismounting.

Apadana: the stairway to the King

54
55 The Apadana is an immense reception room, 240 feet square, where the Achaemenian kings presided over ceremonies and received the homage of subjugated peoples. Beside each step of the stairways leading into it stands the figure in low relief of a foreign tributary bringing gifts to the king. All the ancient races are represented in this procession, enhanced by sculptured flowers, fronds, and animals.

Armed with spears, bearded, curly-haired warriors seem to keep watch over the place. These are the soldiers of the Imperial Guard. There were ten thousand of them. They were called the "Immortals," for as soon as one was killed a new man stepped into his place.

Chapter Eleven

56 Traveling overland through Persia, one has the grandiose vestiges of fifty centuries of history before one's eyes, together with the carpets of Tabriz, the gold- and silverwork of Isfahan, the domes and minarets of Meshed and Kum. This is Persia's glorious past; at Abadan is her future.

In 1890, while excavating an Achaemenian site on the outskirts of Susa, the French archeologist Jacques de Morgan discovered oil. The "Reports of the French Delegation in Persia," which he drew up in conjunction with his colleagues Mecquenem and Pottier, contained a full account of this discovery, but civilized Europe at the time was less interested in oil than in the marbles and porphyry of ancient Persia. Ten years went by. Then an English businessman, William Knox D'Arcy, who had made a fortune in the gold mines of Australia, took an interest in the affair. In partnership with two Frenchmen and an Armenian, D'Arcy created a financial syndicate and asked for a concession from the Shah of Persia, Mozaffereddin Kajar. The Shah, as it so happened, was very short of money at the time and readily consented. To the D'Arcy group, on May 28, 1901, he sold a 20-year concession for a song: twenty thousand pounds sterling plus 16 per cent of the profits.

Several years elapsed before the D'Arcy group made any headway. Prospecting and drilling operations could not be properly carried out until more financial backing was obtained, with the aid of the British government, from the Burma Oil Company. But soon a more serious obstacle arose: the internal situation in Persia grew so uncertain that it was unwise to go on investing capital with no guarantee but the promise of an Oriental potentate.

The Young Turks of the "Union and Progress" movement were then effectively liberalizing the Imperial regime of the Ottoman Empire, and their influence was making itself felt in Persia, especially among the younger generation. Social unrest increased in the cities, and when the bazaar threw in its lot with the malcontents, the Shah at last (August 5, 1906) signed a new, more liberal constitution. This, it was solemnly declared in the preamble, would remain in effect until the return of the Mahdi—which in Persia means Eternity. Elections were held and a new parliament, the Majlis, was sworn in. This was a step forward; the investments of foreign oil interests were now protected by constitutional law. But a second obstacle lay in the way.

For nearly a century Persia had been the theater of a struggle for domination between Russia and England. Occasionally, after strenuous periods of open rivalry, the two powers would come to a provisional agreement and regularize their antagonism. The Russo-British Convention of August 30, 1907, was the most important agreement signed so far. Taking advantage of the unrest and internal disorder attending the constitutional revolution which had just taken place in Persia, Russia and England divided the country between them. The Russians controlled the five northern provinces, as far as a line running through Isfahan and Yezd. The British tightened their hold on the area around Baluchistan in the southeast. The two zones of influence were separated by a neutral zone in which the D'Arcy concession was located. The time was ripe for a systematic exploitation of the oil fields when, on May 26, 1908, new wells, more promising than any of the others, were discovered at Masjid-i-Sulaiman. The Anglo-Persian Oil Company, formed in 1909 to operate the concession, went to work.

In 1913 Great Britain took a step whose political and military repercussions were to be momentous: it decided to run the Royal Navy on fuel oil. The next step was to secure control of the most important oil fields so far discovered. But too much was at stake for Great Britain to allow its fuel supplies to depend on private sources. So on June 20, 1914, for the price of two million pounds, the Admiralty purchased a controlling interest (52.55 per cent of the shares) in the Anglo-Persian Oil Company. Two government commissioners took their seats on the Board of Directors and at the same time a special contract was signed by which the company undertook to supply every gallon of fuel required by the British fleet. All this was the work of Winston Churchill, who had just assumed his first important government post as First Lord of the Admiralty.

From then on the British government directly controlled the South Iranian concessions and worked them in its own way. But other oil fields had now been discovered, and a ruthless struggle began to gain control over them. In 1916 a Georgian businessman, A. M. Khostharia, acquired prospecting and drilling rights in the five northern provinces. The Russo-Persian Naphtha Company which he then formed had only an ephemeral existence, falling a victim to the Bolshevik revolution. But Khostharia shrewdly succeeded in selling his concession for one hundred thousand pounds to the Anglo-Persian Company, which in 1920 founded a subsidiary to run it, the North Persian Company. But in the following year, by a treaty signed on January 26, 1921, the Soviet government formally renounced all the privileges held in Persia by Czarist Russia, and thereby invalidated whatever rights Khostharia had claimed.

With the Russians out of the running for the time being, a new contender appeared on the scene. In 1928 Standard Oil, a subsidiary of the Rockefeller group and eternal competitor of the British companies, obtained a concession in northern Persia under the name of Amiranian Oil Company (American-Iranian Oil Company). Shortly afterward—no doubt quite by chance—Iran abrogated the British concession in the south. This brought about the first Anglo-American compromise in the Middle East: the Americans agreed to renounce the Amiranian concession and received in exchange the right to exploit the oil fields of Saudi Arabia, where they founded the company known as Aramco. The British thereby preserved their petroleum monopoly in Iran and induced the Imperial government to renew the Anglo-Iranian concession in 1933; this contract was supposed to remain in effect until 1993.

The Second World War provided both the Russians and the Americans with a fresh opportunity of securing a foothold in Iran. The Red Army moved into Iran's northern provinces, and Moscow took advantage of the situation to solicit, or rather demand, an oil concession. This maneuver was parried thanks to the efforts of a nationalist deputy, Dr. Mossadegh, who pushed through Parliament a bill forbidding the government from granting any oil concessions as long as foreign troops were stationed on Iranian soil. When the Russians consented to withdraw their troops in March 1946, they did so on the understanding that the north Iranian oil fields would be jointly exploited by Russia and Iran. But Parliament, when it met in 1947, repudiated this agreement made under duress, and the Russians were left empty-handed.

This continual tug-of-war and clash of interests, embittered by press campaigns and parliamentary maneuvers, finally created in Iran an atmosphere of hostility against all foreign oil companies, regardless of nationality. The liberal terms granted by Aramco to the government of Saudi Arabia—profit sharing on a fifty-fifty basis—excited the envy of the Iranian government, which received a much smaller share of the profits realized by the Anglo-Iranian Company.

The British policy consisted in periodically settling its accounts with Iran and, at the same time, confirming the terms of the contract. This was the procedure followed in 1920 and 1932. An attempt was made to apply it again in 1949, but with a slight difference. This time a draft agreement was signed between the Anglo-Iranian Company and the Saed government. Presented as an amendment to the 1933 contract, it recognized the fact that new conditions justified an increase in Iran's share of the profits; but while the royalties were raised from four to six shillings per ton, the gold clause guaranteeing the monetary value of the payments made to Iran was struck out of the contract.

In other words, underestimating the force of popular resentment gathering momentum against it, the British company failed to realize the necessity of making a real sacrifice in order to retain its privileges. It thought that once again, as so often in the past, the Iranians could be bullied into accepting whatever terms were imposed on them. But this time the old methods miscarried. And when at last, alarmed at the agitation breaking out all over the country, the company finally offered to share the profits fifty-fifty, it was too late. The one man who had courageously defended the old agreement with the Anglo-Iranian Company, General Razmara, was assassinated. Twenty-four hours later the Iranian Parliament unanimously voted to nationalize the oil industry. The stage was set for the star performer, Dr. Mossadegh.

From the time he came to power in April 1951, Mossadegh made a point of surrounding his every action with a halo of prophecy. It was he who pushed through the nationalization bill by telling a spellbound Parliament of the voices he had heard and the visions he had seen the night before: "A white form appeared and cried, 'Stand up, Mossadegh, go burst the chains of the Iranian people!'" From then on he posed as the Messiah, in a country where people think of nothing else but the coming of the Messiah.

No trick or subterfuge was too crude for him. One day he solemnly handed over his last will and testament to the representatives of the nation, "in case," he said, "I get assassinated by the enemies of the people." Another time he set up his bed in the House of Parliament.

His swoonings, his tearful harangues, his blatant threats and, it must be said, his (for a time) almost unbroken series of diplomatic triumphs, earned him the title of Man of the Year in the United States in 1951. The striped pajamas in which he appeared time and again became the very symbol of Iranian nationalism. Even his bed became world famous.

His bed, as a matter of fact, proved to be his downfall. He himself was surprised, or pretended to be surprised, at the oddity of his situation. "Has the world ever seen the like?" he said. "A Prime Minister imprisoned in his bedroom for two years!" Locked in his own home, he had lost practically all contact with the people. Add to this the overweening pride of the man. When hostile demonstrations were already taking place in the streets and his empire was tottering, he confidently boasted, "Never mind the mob, they've always been on my side."

He very quickly acquired a taste for absolute power. But he seems to have lacked the courage of his ambition. Then, too, there appears to have been a streak of sadism in his behavior. Under the former Shah he had been imprisoned at Sirjan, and was released only thanks to the good offices of the heir apparent (the present sovereign). His whole policy, once he had assumed power, seems to have been calculated to take revenge on his benefactor. Mossadegh had spent the first half of his life in restless insecurity. Once at the head of the government, he took delight in making life uncomfortable for others.

Toward his ministers he showed the most withering contempt. He treated them like so many menials. It was not unusual for him, when visitors were present, to ask one of his cabinet members to bring him a glass of water or to pass the sugar. The following anecdote is significant in this respect. One day Hossein Fatemi, his minister of foreign affairs, submitted a file of documents to him, relating to business in hand. "It's perfectly absurd!" cried Mossadegh, without so much as looking at them. When his minister tried to explain their contents, the peevish old man seized the sheaf of papers and hit him over the head with them.

If his enemies are to be believed, Mossadegh's behavior was the outcome of physical ailments. Some regarded him as a cyclical lunatic. Others laid stress on the venereal disease with which his family was tainted, and it is a fact that two members of it had to be interned. But whatever the explanation, the truth is that few men could have been more ill-equipped than Dr. Mossadegh to play the part that fell to him. An upper-middle-class Liberal (with royal blood in his veins), he threw himself into a policy of social demagoguery and strictly state-controlled economy.

A wealthy man himself, he did his best to ruin the great property holders. With a thoroughly European cultural background, he tried to cut off Iran from all contact with the West.

In 1944, as a member of Parliament, Mossadegh was instrumental in thwarting the Russian scheme for obtaining control of the north Iranian oil fields. In 1951 he raved and ranted against Great Britain. The assassination of General Razmara threw him into the limelight, in the center of the stage. He seized his opportunity and launched his great venture: the nationalization of Iran's oil fields.

Now while it is true that Dr. Mossadegh had a profound insight into the minds and hearts of his countrymen, the fact remains that he knew nothing whatever about two things on which international politics today largely depend: (1) the structure of the oil industry and (2) the American mentality.

When he canceled their contract and booted the British out of Iran, Mossadegh never for a minute doubted that he would find plenty of customers willing and eager to buy his oil. But he was wrong. There could be no question of making a deal with the Russians. To cut off the West from Iran's tremendous oil resources and put them at the disposal of the Soviet Union might have meant war; the Russians themselves were well aware of this and made no attempt to intervene. Mossadegh may have expected the United States to buy his oil, and buy it on his own terms. But again he miscalculated. His National Front government, when it took power, undoubtedly had the blessing of certain American interests. But the pressure of the mob behind him soon compelled Mossadegh to adopt so violent an "anti-imperialist" policy that he completely alienated American sympathy. And the more he committed himself to extreme nationalism, the more he depended on the mob.

He failed to realize, too, that all the great American oil companies that might have taken the place of the Anglo-Iranian were bound by contractual agreements with the British companies. For a time Mossadegh nursed the hope that, with the support of the Truman administration, he might get his oil industry back on its feet again, but with the Republican victory in 1952 his illusions were shattered.

From then on he was a condemned man. As his power waned, his isolation became obvious. Outside Iran, both the British and Americans were now determined to get rid of the "sinister old man"; within the country itself, royalists, military men, *mollahs*,

and wealthy property holders were now all leagued against him. His last resource was the Tudeh, the Iranian communist party, which was ready to defend his government at all costs. The communist leaders sent out the call to arms and put their sections on an emergency footing. But for a man of the upper middle class like Mossadegh, any solution was preferable to a victory won with the support of the extreme left wing.

What Mossadegh had attempted to do was to push through a revolution without resorting to revolutionary methods, seconded by men devoid of political conviction. That his experiment could be carried out at all was due to the popular sympathies he enlisted by waving the red flag of foreign imperialism. But the truth is that he himself never had any real sympathy with the masses. This being so, he preferred to step aside rather than carry on under their protection.

With Mossadegh gone, things returned to normal. On March 8, 1954, a consortium was formed in London between eight major oil companies: two British (Shell and Anglo-Iranian, henceforth known as British Petroleum), five American (Standard Oil of New Jersey, Socony Vacuum, Standard Oil of California, Gulf Oil, and Texas Oil), and one French (Compagnie Française des Pétroles). Shares were distributed as follows: 52 per cent held by the British, 42 per cent by the Americans, 6 per cent by the French. Negotiations were then opened with Iran and on September 19, 1954, the consortium signed an agreement with the Iranian government and the National Iranian Oil Company.

By the terms of this agreement, valid for twenty-five years, the oil industry in Iran is acknowledged to be state-controlled, in conformity with the nationalization law. The National Iranian Oil Company disposes outright of 12.5 per cent of the total oil production; the profits accruing from the remaining 87.5 per cent are divided equally, half and half, between Iran and the consortium. Iran has furthermore pledged itself to pay the sum of twenty-five million pounds to the Anglo-Iranian Company (now British Petroleum), over a period of ten years, by way of compensation for nationalized property and installations.

But nationalism is on the march. Not only is Iran determined to make the most of its 12.5-per-cent share of the oil produced in the south, but the Tehran authorities have begun prospecting on their own initiative, in an effort to exploit whatever oil resources may be discovered elsewhere in the country.

A government contract was signed in April 1957 with the National Italian Petroleum Administration, run by the famous Enrico Mattei, for the exploitation of certain Iranian oil fields on the basis of a business partnership, which is expected from now on to take the place of the fifty-fifty division of profits hitherto imposed by the great international cartels.

In 1950, the year before nationalization, Persia, with its 32 million tons, ranked fourth among the oil-producing countries of the world, after the United States, Venezuela, and the Soviet Union. By 1956, with 26 million tons, it had dropped back to seventh place, three Arab countries (Kuwait, Saudi Arabia, and Iraq) having now overtaken her. But her oil production is on the rise once more, and the political situation seems to be working in Iran's favor. If nationalism becomes too intense and intransigent elsewhere, the West may prefer to concentrate on Iran's immense oil resources.

Iran's three great refineries can handle 82,000 tons of oil a day, a capacity larger than that of France and equal to that of all the other countries of the Near East combined. Iran's cracking plants (cracking is a process in which the complex hydrocarbons of crude petroleum are converted by heat and pressure into the lighter hydrocarbons that go into commercial gasoline) can handle 19,000 tons a day, twice as much as all the rest of the Near East put together.

Abadan: the modern Persepolis

57
58
The resemblance is striking: the great steel chimneys of the Abadan refinery, only a few miles away from the ancient capital of the Achaemenians, brings to mind the columns of the Apadana. In the starlit nights of Khuzistan, the glittering lights of the oil installations recall the illuminations which so much delighted Sir John Chardin at Isfahan three centuries ago. Oil gushed out for the first time at Masjid-i-Sulaiman, almost on the spot where Zoroaster's temple of fire once stood.

Abadan is the youngest city in Iran, a country which has seen cities come and go, rise and decline, for five thousand years. At the very top of the Persian Gulf, separated from Khuzistan by an arm of the Shatt-al-Arab, on an island quite deserted half a century ago stands now one of the world's largest oil refineries. The city itself offers nothing of any particular interest to the sightseer. The bulk of the popula-

tion consists of one hundred and fifty thousand nomads who, attracted by good pay, have given up the wanderer's life and settled down. They provide the refinery with man power, and Iran with a new proletariat increasingly conscious of its force.

In the midst of this bleak landscape, under the heat of a devastating sun, the British employees of the oil company have built themselves a trim colonial town of neat, cool cottages and gardens that flower all year round, criss-crossed with clean streets straight as a die, and bordered by clear-water canals. The contrast with the native quarters of the old Persian towns could not be more complete. Everything it has done to provide decent housing, hospitals, cooperative stores, restaurants, and in general a pleasant mode of life, is certainly to the oil company's credit.

Abadan: symbols of wealth

59 Since the Mossadegh crisis of 1951, Iran has only very slowly regained its place among the world's great oil producers. In 1956 the royalties paid by the consortium amounted to 146 million dollars. This money goes, for the most part, to finance Iran's seven-year plan of industrial and agricultural development. Oil, and the wealth it creates, have now become the key factor in the national economy.

Storage tanks at Agha Jari

60 "Struck by the Jinn, the door flew open and to my wondering eyes appeared jars overflowing with treasure...."

The tale of Aladdin has become reality. His magic lamp is like a symbol of the eternal combustion of oil.

In the fourth century A.D. the Latin historian Ammianus Marcellinus wrote: "The great mass of the peasantry go the way their overlords drive them, as if doomed to eternal servitude, unencouraged by reward or recompense of any kind."

The Iranian people now expect their leaders to raise their standard of living, to provide better food, better schooling, and improved hygiene. These great oil tanks, whose numbers are increasing all over the country, have caused them plenty of trouble and raised plenty of new problems. But perhaps the worst is over now.

61
62
The Shatt-al-Arab at Abadan

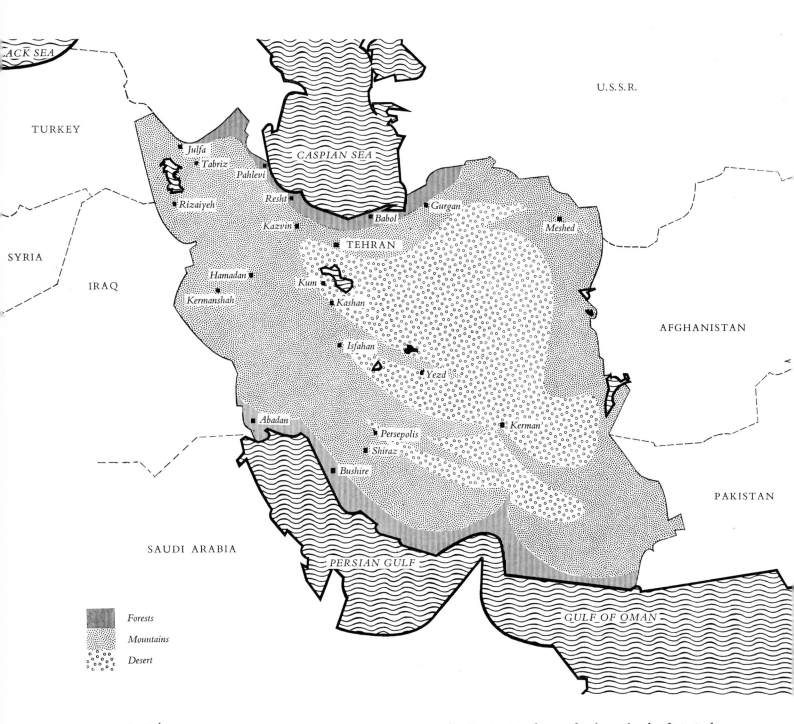

Agriculture

Eighty-five per cent of the population depend for their livelihood on stock farming and agriculture, and occupy about forty-five per cent of Iran's total land area; the rest is high mountains and desert.

The chief agricultural provinces are those around the Caspian Sea, famous for the orchards of Rizaiyeh and Khorasan. Besides fruit, especially citrus fruit, the staple products are rice, tea, cotton, and olives. Mulberry bushes thrive in northern Iran, and this region owes an appreciable share of its income to the silk industry. Wheat, grapes (exported in the form of raisins), and fine tobacco are grown in Azerbaijan.

Smaller areas around the oases lend themselves to fruit growing, and when carefully tended produce apricots, almonds, peaches, cherries, apples, and pears. Vineyards thrive all over the country on the plateaux and in the mountain valleys, and several Persian wines are famous (Shiraz, Kazvin, Zagros).

But wheat is Iran's staple product (2,700,000 tons a year). Enough cereals are grown to satisfy internal needs.

Cotton is the country's second largest export item. Tea and sugar are not produced in sufficient quantities to meet the demand; Iran has to import two-thirds of her sugar and over half of her tea. And tea is the national drink.

Mention must also be made of the ten million or so date palms, along the Persian Gulf, whose yield is by no means a negligible item.

Less profitable but more representative of the country is the growing of special tobaccos for the narghile (or hookah) and of poppies (some 75,000 acres), whose yield of opium is exported largely for medical purposes. The forests of the Elburz range provide several varieties of precious wood, in particular the famous white poplar of Persia, or *tabrizi;* the forests also yield gum tragacanth and dyes (indigo, madder, henna).

Livestock

A land of nomads scattered over vast steppes, Iran depends still today on an essentially pastoral economy. Most important of all is sheep raising (16 million head), followed by goats and cattle (10 million head), horses (2 million) and donkeys (1,200,000). The number of camels (less than 200,000) has decreased sharply in the past few decades owing to the introduction of motor vehicles. Pig breeding (some 30,000 head), strictly forbidden to Moslems, is carried on by a few Armenian farmers.

Forests

There are about 44 million acres of forest land, for the most part in the mountain valleys of Kurdistan and Luristan and on the slopes of the Elburz range in northern Iran. But walnut trees, oaks, white poplars, pines, maples, and plane trees have now been felled on so large a scale that some provinces (Fars province, for example) once thickly wooded are now reduced to scrub and brushwood heaths.

Fisheries

Iran's geographical position gives it access to two very different fishing grounds: (1.) The Caspian Sea, where from 7000 to 10,000 tons of fish are caught annually—chiefly sturgeon, which yield about 30 tons of caviar a year. (2.) The Persian Gulf, which lies too far from Iran's main centers of consumption to be of much importance to the national economy. A small canning industry at Bandar Abbas produces 120 tons of sardines and tuna a year.

Industry

The birth and growth of Iranian industry (chiefly textiles and foodstuffs) dates only from about 1930.

Isfahan is the center of the cotton industry (17,500 spindles), though there are important cotton mills also at Shiraz and Shahi. But their combined production (24 million yards of cotton a year) meets only about one-fifth of the national demand. The rest has to be imported.

The annual output of woolen goods is very much smaller (only 2.2 million yards).

There are 16 flour mills, 7 sugar refineries, tea and tobacco mills, distilleries, and glass works (the latter still a handicraft rather than an industry). Cement works have been founded and are steadily developing.

Since 1955 the importation of industrial equipment has been duty-free. Since April 1956 foreign profits on capital invested in industry can be freely withdrawn from the country.

The second Seven-Year Plan

Inaugurated in 1956, Iran's second Seven-Year Plan provides for investments totaling 930 million dollars, including 175 million in industry alone (for the development of the mining industry first of all, but also of cotton mills, sugar refineries, oil plants, and watch-case factories).

A major item of the plan is a 63-million-dollar hydroelectric dam on the Karaj River, near Tehran, whose 200 million cubic meters of water will generate 110,000 kilowatts of electric power and irrigate the surrounding countryside. A 38-million-dollar dam is being built on the Sapirud River; it will irrigate 290,000 acres and produce 80,000 kilowatts. Smaller dams are being built on the Duruzdan, the Saveh, and the Lar. The Karun Project, in Khuzistan, provides for the irrigation and electrification of two and a half million acres.

11/8/60